THE BLIND HEALER

By the same author

(all published by Terra Nova Publications)

Healing at the Well
Let Healing Flow, Lord
Trust Yates!
Find the Way
Heaven's Dynamite
The Passion to Heal
Christian Healing: Everyday Questions and
   Straightforward Answers
Rediscovering Kingdom Healing
Pilgrimage

THE BLIND
HEALER

MIKE ENDICOTT

MONARCH
BOOKS

Oxford, UK & Grand Rapids, Michigan, USA

First published in the UK in 2011 by Monarch Books
(a publishing imprint of Lion Hudson plc)
Wilkinson House, Jordan Hill Road, Oxford OX2 8DR, England
Tel: +44 (0)1865 302750 Fax: +44 (0)1865 302757
Email: monarch@lionhudson.com
www.lionhudson.com

ISBN 978 0 85721 054 8 (print)
ISBN 978 0 85721 187 3 (epub)
ISBN 978 0 85721 186 6 (Kindle)
ISBN 978 0 85721 188 0 (PDF)

Distributed by:
UK: Marston Book Services, PO Box 269, Abingdon,
Oxon, OX14 4YN
USA: Kregel Publications, PO Box 2607, Grand Rapids,
Michigan 49501

The text paper used in this book has been made from wood independently certified as having come from sustainable forests.

British Library Cataloguing Data
A catalogue record for this book is available from the British Library.

Printed and bound in the UK by Clays Ltd, St Ives plc.

*To my best friend Ginnie,
my wife, my support and my sounding-board.*

Contents

Acknowledgments

My thanks to Peter Byron Davies for his gracious permission to reprint extracts from my writings previously published by Terra Nova Publications. And to Dave Roberts for his excellent editing advice.

Among many others, I must also extend my heartfelt thanks to JB and Ellen Mallay, and Pastor Casey Jones, of Houston, Texas and to Larry Mitchell of Saskatchewan, Canada for believing in this kingdom teaching and promoting its ministry across North America.

Introduction

To be crucified means, first, the man on the cross is facing only one direction; second, he is not going back; and third, he has no further plans of his own.

A. W. TOZER (in *On Being Crucified in Christ*)

I spent the first forty-eight years of my life doing almost exactly the opposite! Far from looking only one way, I searched every avenue for promotion and advancement in life. Even with dimming eyesight, I reached the dizzy heights of being the youngest manager in a huge manufacturing concern. I prided myself on my own strength and courage, which I, somewhat foolishly, imagined to be the sole source of my success.

As for "not going back", I was finding my memories a constant source of joy. Encroaching blindness left me with only the pictures and sounds of bygone, youthful days when I was able to do things that a young man can and should do. As my vision failed, the need grew to spend more and more moments reflecting on those wonderful times. All the things I had seen and the places I had been to were logged away for safe keeping in the album of my memory. All were lovingly revisited as often as possible.

From God, I only wanted one thing – my physical healing. As my life in manufacturing industry grew more and more difficult to cope with, it seemed that a good, solid piece of eyesight-healing intervention from God might allow me to go back to a "successful" lifestyle.

As for "having no plans of his own", I had lots of them! With the growing awareness that my deteriorating sight would not sustain me in industrial management for the rest of my working life, I tried all sorts of things.

I had a go at pottery, writing and gardening, even toying with the idea of photography and painting. I was offered the possibility of becoming a magistrate, and I put myself forward for training for ordination in the Anglican Church, as well. All was to no avail. None of these plans came to fruition; not one seemed to satisfy.

The black day dawned when I had completely run out of plans. I had very little eyesight left, no career prospects, and most of my lovely memories were fading with the approach of middle age.

The firm I worked for was cutting back heavily on staff, and my own personal productivity was going speedily downhill as each month passed. My sight began to go more rapidly. I was in trouble and had nowhere to go. My vision of a perfect, ideal life was fading. I ran very hard into the brick wall of reality.

However, it's often when the ideal meets the real that

exploration truly begins. In sheer desperation, I asked Jesus Christ to take over. Having spent most of my life as a churchgoer brought up in the faith, I now became a Christian in the New Testament definition of the word. I became a disciple of the Son of God – a "student" of the Lord Jesus Christ.

There was so much to learn, and so much to un-learn. There followed a battle of gigantic proportions as I fought to understand how it was that, as the church had always taught me, God was good and yet, despite the loving prayers and ministry of many friends, my healing never came.

However, God had his own ideas. At the foot of the cross of his Son, he exchanged all my wounds and sore places for his abundant peace. That place has since become a haven for me – somewhere for a wounded soldier to lie down.

And lying there, I found the kingdom of God at work. It seems that everything flows from our learning the patience to stand under the cross of Jesus, because when we are there we see what he sees – the infinite glory and love of the Father. That is where the healing fountains start...

CHAPTER 1
Miracles in the Morning

She was limping badly.

I had asked if anyone in the meeting with a stiff joint was prepared to come and see my wife, Ginnie, and me for prayer. I had been teaching a healing, restoring kingdom of grace to 300 avid listeners for the past hour. The time had come for me to take the risk.

"We talk about the grace of Calvary. Now let us show you."

Ginnie and I climbed down from the platform. We wanted to avoid any sense of spiritual showmanship. I stood to the left of the stage, still wearing a microphone and in full view of the expectant crowd. There was a silent pause. Suddenly, I was aware of the lady who had quietly limped up and was standing in front of us.

"I have a painful leg and back," she told us, loudly enough for the whole auditorium to hear her through the microphone mounted on my left ear.

She told us about an accident in her home some twenty years earlier that had left her foot dangling from the end of her leg by only a thread of skin. The surgeons had stitched it back into place and reinforced the ankle by driving a steel rod up inside the leg bone and down through the ankle into the heel. It had grown strong enough to hold her weight again but the ankle was locked rigid by the steel insert. At least she was walking again!

One hot summer, fifteen years later, she was having a tree cut down in her garden and a large part of it fell heavily across that same leg. It snapped the bone halfway between knee and ankle and bent the steel rod in the process.

The bone healed but now the foot was angled and the leg was significantly bowed. Her knee, hip and lower back were plagued with pain because of the appalling posture caused by the bent leg and the consequently twisted foot.

We had long ago learned that heaven responds to two main doors being opened in our souls, one labelled "expectancy" and one labelled "thanksgiving". Jesus often referred to "faith" as a major ingredient to receiving healing, a word we were reinterpreting as "expectancy" to ensure a proper understanding of the sense of trust he was calling for. Psalm 50 had taught us that it is thankfulness that honours God and prepares the way for him to show us his salvation, to show us what had been won on the cross. So we always encouraged thankfulness for the work of Calvary. It is there on the cross, after all, that Jesus took all our pain and carried all our sickness. By his wounds we are healed.

The audience, who were hearing every word of

explanation and ministry, held their collective breath in total silence as we prayed. As they watched her walking back to her seat, the entire auditorium erupted in worshipful cheering and clapping.

I had not been aware that while we were standing with her, giving glory to the Father for the work of the Son, her leg, steel rod and bone had wobbled and shaken and straightened up. She had felt nothing of this divine intervention, but when she began to walk back through the hall she found she could swivel her ankle as well. The following day the lady with the rod in her leg sought us out to thank us. We had done precious little but she wanted us to know how good this pain-free life had suddenly become for her.

There was, we discovered a while later, a full range of movement restored to her foot, although, as we could see from her X-rays, the now straightened rod was still in place! Here again was one of the most fascinating aspects of divine healing. Unusual things often happen that defy all scientific explanation. And yet everyone had seen it.

It put me in mind of someone else who had come for ministry, in a wheelchair and with a badly leaking heart-valve. She has since returned to full-time employment, plays tennis regularly and often goes cycling and jogging. She also takes part in fun-runs and half-marathons. She told me later that her surgeon was bewildered by all this activity, as all his tests were proving that the valve was still leaking!

An hour before this deeply encouraging ministry time, the lights had burned on to the raised platform, the music had died away and the conversations around the hall had hushed. Ginnie and I had stood holding hands, a little way back from the edge of the platform, staring into the glare of the stage lighting. A row of brilliant suns arranged along a gantry the length of the stage and high above the heads of the front row cast a glaring yellow light, hot and dazzling, over us, blotting into darkness most of those who sat expectantly before us in the auditorium.

We stood there holding hands and smiling, grinning at the unseen audience in front of us and grinning at each other. We were thrilled just to be there! It had taken ten months for us to step up on to this particular platform, ten months since the original invitation came, ten months since I wrote the fastest acceptance I had ever written. This was a speaking job I really wanted, but then I want all of them.

The vicar who had been praying for us seconds before jumped down from the stage and took a seat in the front row. We were on our own. I could feel all 300 audience members watching us; I could feel their anticipation matching our own. We had arrived where we had wanted to stand for such a long time and felt very much at ease. We were about to do what we feel most comfortable doing.

We were about to teach them the great news of Christ's intent, since Calvary, for his church to be proclaimers of his saving, healing grace to this pained and broken world.

They were eager to hear. We knew that the dynamics of the kingdom of God were present to heal – they always are – and we were ready to give glory to our God for it.

"Good morning!" I looked around, grinning at them.

"Good morning," came the reply – quiet, hesitant, half-hearted and perhaps a little insecure. These dear people seemed unsure of what they had let themselves in for. A blind man with a healing ministry? These healing conferences are, as they say, "two-a-penny" in that neck of the woods. But they had come, nevertheless.

But their quiet hesitation might have been something else; in this part of the world public speakers on healing ministry often come direct from jazzy TV shows, with mixed, and sometimes fearful, reputations. Audiences like this one often have an unspoken fear that they may be pushed unceremoniously over on to their backs if they so much as approach the platform for help and come within arm's length of the speaker!

Either that, or they suspect they may be called upon to reach for their wallets. So they hold their breath. They wait. They let the speaker prove what sort of a showman speaker he is before they begin to ease themselves into the proceedings. So right away it was time to put my cards on the table and break down the barriers.

"Now," I told them, "it seems that we might have a problem here. You see, I need you to react to me as I speak to you. OK?"

I could have cut the silence with a knife. What were they expecting? But I was smiling inside; this method of introducing myself has its practical advantages, for sure, but it's also a wonderfully effective ice-breaker.

"So," I went on, "I need you to shout out how you feel about what I have to say to you. Any time you feel like it! Shouts like 'Alleluia!' would be just fine. 'Amen!' is good and 'Preach it to them, brother!' is even better. Even the odd shout of 'Heresy!' will help things along here."

Some of them sounded as if they were chuckling at that, a sure sign that they might be beginning to relax, so I thought it best to tell them why I needed them to respond to me in this way.

"I need you to respond" – I was trying now to speak in smiling mock authority – "so that I know you are still here! You see, I can't see. If you just sit there in complete silence for the next hour or so, how am I to know that you haven't just all crept silently away and I'm not standing here addressing an empty auditorium?"

This last statement was greeted with gales of laughter. Everyone in the room was relaxing now as they realized there would be no pretence on this platform, no acting, no pretending to be anything I am not. The barriers had all come tumbling down.

I had come to talk to them about the dynamics of the living and growing kingdom of God – and that, I constantly remind myself, is no place to play around with audiences. Kingdom business is serious business.

I had already lost far too many nights of sleep, trying to hunt down an understanding of why it might be that our beloved Christian church has allowed such a decline in her healing ministry.

"It used to work marvellously," I told them, "but now it doesn't work nearly so well. What a shame! Everywhere I walk in life – home, the office, the street, holidays, work times – everywhere I walk is among the sick, the ill, the diseased and the dying. It'll be the same for you if you look around you!

"Worryingly, we seem sometimes to know almost nothing of kingdom dynamics after two thousand years. If we did, then we would all be workers of miracles like our spiritual forefathers. Allowing our healing ministry to go on drifting further and further away from the purity and dynamic, effective nature of its original form is killing off our involvement in producing the fruit of the kingdom."

Ever since, our response has been to try to pour more and more additional skills from the worlds of medicine, psychology and social work – and even figments of our own imaginations! – into the healing ministry.

"For some reason we, as a church, seem determined that the cross needs to be added to, but in fact," I emphasized excitedly, "it doesn't need us to add anything at all to it. If only we could take the risk and rely on the cross's work, it works wonderfully as it is!

"Think about it. Would it not be marvellous if the local non-believers could say to each other, 'Let's go up to that church where people get healed!'?"

It was crossing my mind to suggest, on that blindingly bright platform, that unbelievers probably care very little about what we believe in. Like a lot of the people listening to me, I have been "nice" at church outreach events but it doesn't help that much. Nor does being a good example of wholesome standards in life stand out much. There are plenty of folk out there already, living decent lives, who are not Christians.

My experience of unbelievers tells me that practical power, not more religious theories, is the thing that they are looking for today. They are not, in the main, listening to our attempts at preaching. They have plenty of problems and not enough solutions. They are sick. They are hooked on alcohol and drugs. Their relationships are tearing them apart. It's a mess out there.

I gently challenged the audience to consider how many people they knew over the age of forty who were not on any sort of medication. My request, and the obvious, in-built suggestion that went alongside it, was greeted with knowing smiles and shrugging shoulders. Well, most people, when I ask that question, smile knowingly and shrug their shoulders. Most seem to write off this depressing thought while accepting it as the price of our living longer, but I was suggesting to them that never before has the field been so ready for harvest, so ripe for the display of God's kingdom grace.

The modern world has turned the lives of so many

unbelievers upside down, to such an extent that many have no idea where to go, or what to do, to get their lives put back together again.

"I don't think that they really care very much at all if we Christians pray in tongues or dance up and down in the aisles or stand to attention with stiff military precision and sing out of a hymnal. But if only you and me, the people of God, had a ministry that could get their bodies healed and their lives straightened out, I feel pretty sure they would come to wherever we are. Not only that, but they would start to listen to what we have to say."

There were some encouraging murmurings of "Amen" from around the room.

"I have been convinced for a while in the depths of my soul," I explained to my audience, who were by now somewhat taken aback by this forthright introduction, "that God wants his church to have the same reputation today that Jesus had during his earthly ministry. Come to think of it, perhaps he has always wanted that. I reckon he wants people to say the same sort of things about us that they must have said to each other about those first-generation disciples. They would have noticed that the power of God was at work in believers!"

I was pressing the point, now, into the quiet and dark abyss in front of me.

"All this means to the general public out there is that the gospel without power does not sound particularly like good news to them. You and I, the already-converted ones, know full well that it is, because it brings salvation, but it doesn't look like that to outsiders.

"Given the seemingly random effects of the fall, they have great needs in their minds and their bodies. When they get hurt it all seems so unfair to them. If the only thing we Christians have to give folk is a nice new set of rules to live by and a new set of standards to live up to, teaching them a mode of life without really changing their lives, what good have we done for them?" I demanded.

I was thinking that if we are not careful, we merely bind them up with another set of "shoulds" and "should nots", another set of rules.

"And there is always a real danger," I added, feeling now that I had really caught their attention, "that we Christians might look like a little huddle of pious people, shutting our doors against the world, connoisseurs of liturgy, lost in prayer and praise, congratulating each other on the excellence of our Christian experience.

"But if only we were willing to take a risk and deal with the sick in the way that Jesus taught and practised, then we would be doing again an important part of what God sent us to do. As people watch what we do, they would listen to what we have to say. Then it is possible they might begin to care about what we believe in."

But, I badly needed them to understand, all this would mean that we must be a living example of God's power at work. Our ministry has to do what it says on the tin.

"People today are not so excited by religious theories as we might have been a thousand years ago, or even a hundred years ago! Today's worldly general public are not overawed and drawn in by high ritual or by any practices at all that don't come up with significant and measurable results. We need to see a ministry with tangible consequences, with the earthly ministry of Jesus and the apostles as our model."

Someone gave a lively shout of "Alleluia!" and someone else shouted, "Amen!" – and we were on the way. Things were livening up. The conference had begun.

There's an old apple tree behind our house, I told them, which gives a small crop every year, right at the end of long, waving branches and way out of reach. It hasn't been pruned even once in all the years we have lived there!

The church's ministry to the sick had grown like that apple tree – unpruned, unchecked, for centuries. New methods have added to the cross in its simplicity, all creating longer and longer branches and less and less fruit. Things look very different, I was explaining, in a commercial apple orchard. Here the trees are pruned, kept short, kept accessible, loaded down with fruit begging to be picked. The pruning back to the basics that Jesus taught, the simple kingdom truths he taught the disciples, would give the whole church a really effective ministry again – a divinely designed one!

When I eventually stumbled upon this original

ministry of Jesus, I had decided I would call it "kingdom healing" to distinguish it from other methods. It would probably be unrecognizably different, centred as it would be on what Christ came to do – to proclaim the kingdom and secure an open door for its work when he died on the cross.

For the previous eight years or so, I had been seeking to understand Christ-taught kingdom healing and how to apply it in real and effective and reliable kingdom restoration. I was just beginning to understand what to say to a crowd like this about kingdom dynamics.

Here in front of me were 300 questing souls, every single one of them with a different understanding of and hugely complicated questions about healing and restoration. Jesus had been able to simply teach these principles to fishermen and tax collectors. What was once simple has become frighteningly varied and complicated as we have sought to "improve" it.

The ordinary people at that conference just wanted to put their hope in and persevere with something simple that works.

I stood in front of them, thrilled to be with them, thrilled at the knowledge of what I was going to say to them, thrilled at the prospect of seeing the kingdom at work yet again, and thrilled at the thought of their being able to "do it" out there in the world for themselves.

I launched myself onwards into my talk. I don't have any notes to work from when I am speaking, since

I can't see them, but I hold five or six subject headings in my head and simply work from one heading to the next, relying on previous experiences and past "trial and error" to carry me through an hour's talking. Like a car driver who can concentrate on navigation and steering, observation, braking and accelerating, but still talk to their passenger or listen to the radio, I keep talking even as my mind prompts me about my next point.

I talked to them about kingdom dynamics for today, framed by the purpose of God's heart to restore all the damage of the fall and his longing to restore the world to the blueprint conditions of Eden. One day it will all be restored in the new city of Jerusalem coming from heaven.

And at the same time, like a car driver conversing with his passengers, I was asking myself the same old questions in my mind as I stood in front of these folk who had come to hear my version of the message of the cross.

But why were we, the church, letting them down so badly? When Jesus had told us not to fear, because it is the Father's good pleasure to give us the kingdom, why then did we insist on putting blocks in people's way? Why were we sowing tares with the wheat? Why were we telling them that God doesn't want to heal everybody, and that their sins were stopping God from healing them, when Jesus had died for the sins of the whole world?

So, by the end of this first conference session, I had enjoyed myself enormously and was desperately hoping, without being able to see their faces and their body language, that the audience were climbing on board.

Ginnie had been jumping up from time to time to join me, reading out the scriptures that showed the apostles, the deacons and everyday, ordinary Christians like us, going about their daily business and healing the sick, witnessing to crowds and seeing thousands coming into the church when they saw the miraculous kingdom life.

She read about Jesus always granting every request for healing and then telling us that he only did the Father's will. She read about power pouring out of Jesus, that there is great power for those of us who believe, and that God doesn't change. She left me to conclude that power is still pouring out of him today for all who come to him with a mustard seed of expectant trust.

By the time the session was over, I knew it was time to make straight a path for Jesus to show them his glory. That's what I did and that's what he did.

The lady with the bent rod in her painful leg was swiftly followed by two other late-middle-aged ladies, friends who were both progressively losing their sight. We prayed for them, and they were both restored by Almighty God through his grace within minutes, according to their on-the-spot testimony. The audience gasped!

By now the church's prayer ministry team were working hard and were all quite shocked and shaken to see so many gifts of grace being poured so freely into the wounded, of whom there are always many. We were, of course, not surprised at all, as we had come to understand, just as the early church did, that as we proclaim the good news of the character of Jesus and the outworking of the cross, then the Holy Spirit will come and confirm what we say with signs and wonders.

It's the way the divine system was originally designed to work, after all.

Soon Ginnie and I were called to help pray with a gentleman in a wheelchair suffering from an aggressive tumour in his brain. His wife had gently wheeled him up and told us he was undergoing, by the sound of it, the maximum dose of every known treatment. That was only in the hope of preventing the evil thing from growing ever larger. His doctors were desperately working to prevent any further growth.

Again, there were no requests to heaven. Kingdom healing, the exciting and effective ministry that Jesus himself exercised and taught, was built another way altogether. The early church had a working relationship with God that led them to realize their role was that of proclamation of the kingdom. Then, when they had done this fully, God would do the healing as confirmation of what they were proclaiming. Jesus never prayed any "please" prayers for the sick and we don't either. Just worship, thanksgiving and praise together with honest, heartfelt, trusting proclamation of the message of the cross.

We heard nothing about the gentleman again for three days, until a phone call came in after his next treatment appointment at the hospital. He was able to report that the tumour had reduced in size by 75 per cent! Two weeks later I heard from his wife that hospital tests couldn't find the tumour any more.

Having prayed with him, Ginnie and I sat down on the edge of the platform to catch our breath and then climbed back on to the stage to close the meeting.

Ginnie lifted up my right hand with a smooth and well-practised movement, placed it lightly on the edge of the lectern, and left the platform. Touching the podium rim was not a superstition – like a footballer only able to play when wearing a pair of lucky boots. It has become a natural, subconscious and discreet movement, developed with unrehearsed practice at many speaking engagements.

It may look very romantic, this couple holding hands on stage, but the reasons are very practical. She places my hand on the lectern edge, which then acts as the needle on a blind man's directional compass. That side edge points me directly down the middle of the auditorium, and that is vital.

We had found ourselves before in churches with no movable lectern and no platform edge and no way to hold the centre line. Without the ability to focus on the crowd, my naturally animated style of teaching can soon cause me to turn slightly sideways, bit by bit, without noticing the movement, and finishing up devoting all my attentions to someone sitting on the far right of the first pew!

Not being able to see, I can so easily lose track of the centre line, as it were, and turn too far one way or the other. It is then that I can hear Ginnie's whispers pushing through my enthusiasm for the work at hand: "Left a bit!"

One church recently had even supplied us with a brass music-stand for this purpose, but it was a light and collapsible model with a revolving top, and the inevitable results were nothing short of hilarious.

But this time we had made sure. The organizers had installed a solid lectern right in the middle, pointing right down the centre aisle, and we were ready to go again.

Then it came. The one question I always dread because, try as I might, there seems to be no answer that will satisfy.

Even after all the evidence from Scripture and the breathtaking works that had unfolded abundantly, through grace, right in front of them all, someone from the depths of the darkened audience still asked the old question, threw the old spear. Here it was again.

"If what you say is true, then why hasn't God healed you?"

I took a deep breath, climbed back on to the stage, and reached into my pocket to switch the microphone back on.

CHAPTER 2
Rock Racing

There must be a hundred different ways of answering that question. I wish there weren't. Naturally, I get asked it a lot.

Two things always bother me about finding the right answer. I am very aware that being blind doesn't look like the greatest witness in the world to the healing God that I preach and demonstrate. I also want to be sensitive to the reality that the question of what is, and what isn't "leading life to the full" is a very personal one.

Checking out John 10:10, I find Jesus talking about this:

> *The thief comes only to steal and kill and destroy; I have come that they may have life, and have it to the full.*

Does "leading a full life" mean being healed of everything because someone else thinks that's the best answer? This raises so many questions.

Of course we would long to see anyone healed of terminal cancer, but how should I react if they want their freckles to disappear? Is that serious enough to trouble God with? Of course we would all want to see an end to mental illness, but what if someone just gets a bit miserable sometimes?

Watching my own feelings over the years about such thorny questions, I have settled on two closely connected views; firstly, that healing seldom occurs where there is little compassion to speak of. Secondly, my own compassion rises dramatically when observing in someone that a part of their lives has taken over the whole. Whether the problem is terminal cancer or freckles, or anything in between, my compassion rises when a part of someone's life rules the rest of it. I am not trying to say that we should not bother God with small things, or that he would not be bothered with them. I am saying only that it's difficult to have a compassionate involvement in other people's needs. We should determine whether or not they are being ruled by something through taking the time to listen to them.

So, on the frequent occasions when the question is asked, I find myself thrown immediately into an internal emotional and spiritual battle. The sting of incursion through private boundaries is easy for a sinner like me to resent. But I'm also aware that a genuine dollop of doubt assails so many because of my blindness, and this doubt needs to be addressed and overcome. In the middle of this momentary fight I begin to weigh up a hundred different answers, all true, but all with slightly different emphases.

I stood there for a moment, as usual, quickly sorting through the options in my mind. I was veering towards the "twenty-five-year rule". I have a theory about human beings that I am comfortable with. When a person has possessed something, pain free, that others might consider they would like to be healed of and they have had it for more than twenty-five years, that aspect of their lives has by then melted into them. It becomes part of their personality. I have gone around that clock twice now and blindness has become part of who I am.

I quite like being who I am and, if it doesn't sound too pompous, I have no wish to change things. Life works very fully for me. I do all the things I want to do and I don't have to do any of the things I do not particularly want to do.

Let me put it another way. There is a great difference between being blind and going blind. If I had lost my sight in an accident recently, then the part would have doubtless taken over the whole and I would be forcing my way to the front of the ministry queue and, perish the thought, pushing everyone out of the way in the process!

I would certainly be that keen to receive my sight. But it has been this way a long, long time and is now built into the essence of who I am.

The lesson I learned about this was reinforced one day when I was teaching at a convent to a group of nuns and others. At the finish of it all, I suggested we pray for each other. One young girl, I suppose in her mid twenties, squealed very loudly and very close behind me. I turned to enquire and discovered that what I understood later to be a birth deformity was being dramatically made whole. Her left foot was apparently much smaller than the other one, but fitted into the same sized shoe with the aid of some polystyrene packing. As her foot grew she began to be in pain as it pressed into the packing. Her left leg was straightening and filling out and the left side of her face was lifting to match the other side. A nun who was praying with her exclaimed, "But, my dear, you're so beautiful!"

But a few minutes later there was pandemonium. When she crossed the front doorstep into the car park to drive home, she lost the healing. People crowded around, shouting at demons or kneeling in fervent prayer. Someone came and fetched me and, when the others had all gone, I asked her what had happened.

"Six months ago," she told me tearfully, "I married the most fabulous man in the whole wide world! When I saw my car here I realized that I was going back to him, and I have to tell you this – I cannot afford to go home any different."

She was making it very clear to me that the way her husband felt about her, and doubtless vice versa, was her idea of her perfect fullness of life. If relationships were only based on what we look like, then heaven help us! She had no wish to risk being in any place that might affect the way he thought about her. At the very least she wanted to talk with her newly wedded husband.

At that very moment I learned that it is not ours to judge what is and what isn't fullness in other people's lives. She might be measuring her own fullness of life differently than you or I might, but it was her life and it wasn't my place to direct or dictate to her. And so I blessed her and let her go, thanking God for such a lesson.

Let me put my blindness in a wider context. Losing my sight has been a gradual affair. It has not been the result of some accident or injury, but the creeping disease known as *retinitis pigmentosa* (known in the eyesight business as RP). The effect of this degenerative complaint is to kill off, usually very slowly, the millions of nerve ends that go together to make up the retina – the light-sensitive part at the back of the eye. The disease is medically incurable, starting at any time in life and working its way relentlessly onwards, until total blindness becomes an inevitable fact of life.

It would be easy to imagine that such a disability would take life over completely, allowing the recipient to be judged by society, if not by himself, as one of life's casualties. Indeed, sympathetic comments made to Ginnie and audience questions often bear this out. But the opposite seems to be true.

Somehow, I have been given a place of victory to live in – a place of peace and love; a place of full kingdom life in which to live and have my being. How did that happen?

When I look back over my life, it looks like a switchback road. It has been full of ups and downs, joys and tears, and I recognize, believe it or not, that the worst times have been the times of greatest blessing.

It has been in the troughs that I have been able to get close to God, rather than on the peaks. It has been in the lowest places that my healing has come. Peering back into the memories of some of the harder times is not as painful as it once was. Many of those valleys of despair are now filled with the healing grace which is found in Jesus Christ, and the picture of the past is now a joyful one.

Of course, it gets depressing sometimes, but again and again God's promise comes back to me. He has promised to be there when I need him. His word assures me that whenever I pass through the waters, he will be with me. I can pass through the rivers and they will not overwhelm me. When I am forced to walk through fire, I will not be burned; and the flame will not consume me (Isaiah 43:1–2). This is all because he is the Lord my God, the Holy One of Israel, my Saviour.

However, as I write and speak about these things, I am only too well aware that there are many who are "worse off" than myself, and who suffer greatly. Others are quite surprised to discover my blindness and decide they are better off than I am, after all. There are some whose pain is temporary, and some who seem to suffer continually. Some are in physical pain and some not. But where the rubber hits the road, the real problem lies at the core where our emotions and attitudes find their root. If we strugglers can find what lies there, and it is usually our sufferings, then God will have a chance to heal us with his grace.

My own journey with blindness unfolded as follows. RP had no effect at all on my early years. I had an almost perfect childhood. My father, a naval officer of considerable standing and ability, had remained in the Navy for many years after the Second World War. Thus it was that I spent my school summer holidays in Malta at a sort of temporary family home, where my mother might see the most of him.

Memories of those days are filled with beach picnics with my mother and sister, learning to roller-skate on disused tennis courts, and children's parties on ships moored in the harbour. There were warm and clear blue bays to swim in, under piercing azure skies; and harmless jellyfish, which provided an endless source of fun-fight missiles.

My first twelve summers meant commuting between London and Malta, from school to paradise, from spoiling grandparents to spoiling summer holidays. Could anyone have wanted more?

My parents had always kept a house in Hampshire, rented out during our travels, and it was to there that I reluctantly returned at the end of our Mediterranean chapters. I use the word "reluctantly" with care, as our English home really was home to me; it contained the security and stability that lies so comfortingly in childhood memories.

After a spell based back in Hampshire, when our father served at Portsmouth, we moved to a tiny village on the South Devon coast, to be within easy reach of Plymouth, where he was now based. School holidays – especially the summer ones – were filled with sailing and canoeing, yacht clubs, parties and so on. I travelled on into my early teenage years, in blissful ignorance of what was to come.

To try to recall now what it was like to see properly is to allow these fondest memories to drift up to the surface. They are brightly coloured pictures of rows of beached sailing boats along the seaweedy yacht club shoreline, with halyards slapping gently against angled masts in the breeze. There are full- colour pictures of rolling green and wooded hillsides, sloping down to blue estuaries and the tiny harbour, with vessels of all shapes, sizes and colours, resting at anchor.

Even now in my memory, I can count the trees along the shoreline and see the wing-tips of the swans as they beat the water: a long line astern of dazzling white bodies, lifting and taking off in the evening light. They would come slapping down the river towards the sea, rippling pools spreading from their wing-tips, like the oars of a university rowing club, as they touched the still evening water.

There was the rowing boat tied up at the bottom

of the estuary steps. Mother had dipped deep into her Post Office account for this wonderful extra. My elder sister, Carolyn, and I remember living in that boat more than we lived indoors. The pleasure it brought us was immeasurable.

Then there came the moments of high excitement, too. Sitting on the cliff edge, in the early dawn light, feet dangling into space, we would search the horizon for that big old, grey naval cruiser – the one bringing our father, returning from a year's absence at sea. Then there were the two of us, flying down the cliff path to home, our feet skimming the rough track, and then the tarmac lane to the cottage. We had seen the ship. Father was on his way, and Mother would have to know that he was here!

These were wonderful times: close to nature, and full of promise. Just around the corner, where the estuary poured into the sea, lay our beach – at least we always thought of it as being ours. This strip of half-sand, half-rock, was only twenty minutes' walk from the cottage, and much used by family and friends at every opportunity.

At each end of the sandy strip lay multitudes of tumbled rocks, crowded in together and raised up at crazy angles, smooth and sharp, high ridges and deep pools. This was the family race track. Carolyn and I would start at one end and race each other headlong across the tops of the boulders, an incredible feat of sharp eye and dancing foot co-ordination. Somehow we never fell, never broke a bone, nor grazed a knee past easy mending.

Rock racing was surely the sport of kings! One of the first things on my list of exciting things which will just have to be done when I get to heaven (after worship) is to go rock racing with my sister Carolyn again. What sport we shall have!

It was not until I reached the age of fifteen or so that I began to notice any effect of the disease, which by then had just begun to take hold. The earliest wondering came when stumbling over my words while reading aloud in the classroom. Bits of words began to go missing, much as they do when one is very tired. But it was enough to trouble me, largely because of my classmates' guffaws.

However, I managed to pass all the requisite examinations – except one. The subject of divinity, as religious education was called in those days, was far beyond me. I had absolutely no interest in the subject at all! Church life at home and chapel life at school were just there because they were there; they were compulsory school and family activities. These lessons were never fought against, merely endured.

By then I was living with an almost permanently bruised nose. I was being regularly and unceremoniously shoved into school notice-boards by so-called "chums", who drew great delight from pushing the back of my head whenever they saw me peering too closely at some school notice or other. They must all have thought this act of teasing to be hilarious, but each amusing shove still lingers in my memory; not because of a failure to forgive but as a hurt from long ago.

I had given up shooting, too. This had been a well of endless pleasure – not killing animals, I should add, but punching little holes in targets a thousand yards away. The school rifle club had a reasonably competitive reputation on the circuit, and I had loved being part of that; it was something at which I was pretty good. But it had to go. Things were getting out of focus, and sometimes I was even hitting the wrong target. Graceful withdrawal, albeit fairly devastating, was the honourable thing to do, before I started letting the team down.

And after school, what to do? Believing that I could be a surveyor – a land agent, as my uncles had been – I set off to London to gain some professional qualifications, and from there to seek my fortune in the world. At what seems now to be the very tender age of seventeen, and with a parental support promise of £10 per week, I packed my bags and set off for the London city lights.

Little by little, every year after that became harder. I had found and married Ginnie, who became a great friend and a stable rock to me, but our life together was being threatened by growing financial difficulties. It became a greater and greater struggle.

The years rolled by and my sight deteriorated still further, and the more I tried to apply my brain to the search for some other future that would be physically possible, the deeper I slipped into a pit of hopelessness. Eventually it felt as though I was a lemming running over a cliff. There seemed to be absolutely nothing that could be done about my situation.

Around that time a friend told a joke about a parachutist whose canopy failed to open, and I remember missing the punchline entirely because I felt such an affinity with the poor man. I still believed that there would be a safety net at the bottom of my decline, but I was not sure what it might be.

Memories of schoolboy Christianity, and a vague and distant memory of a sense of there being some security in religion, sometimes prompted me to turn to the Scriptures for help. Then one Sunday morning I heard a psalm being read on the radio. It suddenly seemed as if a lifebelt had been thrown towards me, and I longed to grasp it firmly, but my insufficient faith prevented it:

> *He lifted me out of the slimy pit, out of the mud and mire; he set my feet on a rock and gave me a firm place to stand.*

> PSALM 40:2

How this help would arrive I had no idea, but the falling had gone on long enough.

CHAPTER 3
Demolition

Excitement filled the house. For a week we waited – the lull before the storm. Then the bomb dropped out of a clear blue sky, destroying everything. The rejection letter hit the doormat and my soul went through the floor.

Everything had been planned with success in this process as a given. "Devastation" is not a powerful enough word: "demolition" is nearer. I just went numb. I had done the best I could. I had applied every skill and bit of knowledge I had. Best behaviour had oozed from every pore. I had done my utmost to sound reasonably intelligent.

Total black misery swamped me. I sat on the back doorstep and cried. Days and weeks and months drifted by while, in the depths of emotional unrest and hopelessness, I drove round and round the roundabout of possibilities, discovering that each and every exit in turn was a cul-de-sac. There was no way out, and it hurt.

I had applied to be a minister in the Church of England. It was my Plan B as blindness overtook me.

But I had been rejected.

My youthful apathy towards faith had melted a little and I had slipped into church life in our local village. But before tracing my meandering path towards Jesus, let's fill in the rest of the gaps.

My first wage-earning job, after London, was in the carpet mills in the historic city of Halifax, Yorkshire. There I met the girl I fell in love with, and eventually married over forty years ago. There we settled, but not for long.

Ginnie remembers how I told her, in those far-off days, that I knew that God had a plan for my life. I had no idea what it was going to be. I know now! I would not have called myself a Christian in those days, or even a regular churchgoer, and forgot the idea until company mergers made me redundant.

So we went to Wales, to begin a new career in the car industry. After only a few years we moved to our present lovely home, joined village life and started to attend church regularly, as many do when seeking to put down roots in a new community.

Two children came along in due course but my career was beginning to turn sour. The company was marvellous in keeping me on as long as they could, but failing sight was making life in factories more and more difficult, if not downright dangerous!

By this time I had eventually reached the point where the dreaded fortieth birthday was looming on the horizon – the imaginary halfway point where some men's minds drift longingly into the unreal realms of alternative career moves. I dreamed of becoming a clergyman. Was this what is known as a mid-life crisis?

I could readily see myself in a clerical collar, receiving all the love and respect due to that position and most importantly, being valued for my cerebral strengths rather than being doubted for my physical weaknesses. All the organizational and management skills which I had picked up over the intervening years in the car industry would serve me well. My theology felt pretty sound. Well, it felt as sound as anyone else's. Little did I know!

Had I known then how the gracious Lord was going to turn my life upside down, change most, if not all, of my thinking, reverse most of my outlooks, and then pour blessings into my existence with such abundance, I would never have had the nerve to do what I did. There would have been no need.

I applied for training for ordination in the Anglican Church. The family were more than supportive. The whole matter seemed a very safe option. I could carry on working for my living at the factory and be a priest in my spare time. It's such a disgraceful thought now, but I was starting to be dragged down by life's quicksands. It would have been a wonderful qualification for alternative employment should I ever fall foul of the ever-present and overshadowing threat of losing my position with the company because of increasing loss of sight.

The thought of becoming a priest began to open up

over this falling person, like an all-too-welcome parachute. The redundancy threat was starting to loom and gather like darkening storm-clouds on life's horizon. A period of economic recession, with all its accompanying evils, was catching up on us at my place of work. A company that once prided itself on the security it offered its staff was now in the position of having to provide redundancy programmes for them. This would be a good time to put in a backstop.

My own vicar was thrilled. He set about smoothing the path ahead with church committees, whose approval would have to be sought as a first step. This done, the application went forward to the diocese for the Bishop's approval and I waited anxiously for the call to interview.

In no time at all, I was marching around the park at the rear of the Bishop's house, rehearsing the answers to the most likely questions. "Why do you want to be ordained?" and "What do you feel you can offer the Church?" These were the obvious ones. I wanted the replies to be unhesitatingly smooth and professional.

I guessed that the worst question would be, "How will you manage church services with insufficient sight?" Hoping that the subject would not be raised, I resolved to say something to the effect that God would find a way if he wanted to. After an hour of kicking down brown, crinkled leaves along tarmac paths around the rainy park, the appointed time arrived. And in I went.

To my horror, the interview room was crowded. A

large table almost filled the space from door to window. At the head of it sat the imposing figure of the then Bishop. Along either side were ranged no fewer than eight good men and true, some clergy and some lay, with one empty chair – presumably left for me. I sat down on it, looking around as best I could and praying there were no wet leaves still sticking to my shoes!

Happily, the Bishop, in all his scarlet, was well out of focus at the other end of the grand table, so his presence would not worry me. As for the rest, I had no idea who they were, as all their faces were blurred.

I thought they might all start the meeting by introducing themselves to me, but thankfully that didn't happen. To be bombarded with a broadside of impressive titles would have done nothing to boost my confidence at that moment. The main worry now would be guessing which one was asking the questions. I would have to be looking fairly accurately in the direction of the voice when answering, or it would be clear that I didn't have a clue who was speaking!

Without being able to see lip movements, nor even which particular face was turned towards me, it was becoming so important to pinpoint sound-source direction. In this way I could pretend to look straight back at the right speaker, a technique I was still trying to master, knowing all the while that if I misguessed the direction, I would be answering the wrong person. Would that not look as though something were really wrong? To answer without looking into the face of the questioner seems so rude. It would not take them long to see the size of the problem.

These were the uncertainties that dogged my interview technique. All the pre-interview planning flew out of the window behind me. All that remained was sheer fear. The first enquiry came down the table like a naval broadside, despite all my preparation in the park.

"Could you please tell us all why you wish to be ordained?" Suddenly, I lost sight of them all. The vision which lay before me was that of a flock of vultures, crowding around a dying animal in the bush. This image quickly faded, only to be replaced by a vision of standing on the edge of a lake full of crocodiles, just waiting for me to jump!

I will never know how I came through forty minutes of third-degree grilling. Surely their hearts were all in the right place, but what is received under circumstances like these always outweighs what is given.

I was faintly outraged about the interview process – lots of imposing people bearing down on one single individual – which had been discarded by industry years before. It never really got the best results out of any interviewee. We had long ago opted for a more friendly and informal approach, to get the best out of our job applicants.

So what a lovely surprise it was, a fortnight later, to receive a letter saying that the Bishop and his team had accepted and would support my application. Even if my motives were a bit doubtful, it seemed to me that God wanted this thing to happen anyway, so I looked forward with eagerness to the final hurdle: the National Board. This would involve three days of interview in my nearest theological college.

This was going to be tougher. Here the questions were going to be more searching, more thorough. Two areas needed my attention – both to do with eyesight. What would happen when I lost the little sight I had left? How could I cope with the job from a practical viewpoint and how could I tell people that there was indeed a good God up there somewhere while I was going blind?

This was, undeniably, the first time I began to seriously question the latter. Never before had it even dawned on me that God and a suffering world had anything to do with each other. God was a fairly remote sort of character to me in those days, before the tipping-point of a Midnight Mass that came a year later. Salvation was something that might happen at death if we were lucky and managed to catch God on a good day!

Surely, the national interviewers would want to examine me more closely on these things. So I enlisted the help of a friend to search the Scriptures on the question of eyesight. The very first thing that he came up with was quite earth-shattering, and a lesson I have never forgotten. It read:

> *The Lord said to him [Moses], "Who gave man his*
> *mouth? Who makes him deaf or mute? Who gives*
> *him sight or makes him blind? Is it not I, the Lord?"*
>
> EXODUS 4:11

"Some friend!" I thought. I did not want to know this at all; this was devastating. Here was a God to walk away from, not one to carry into the world. Here was a God who was directly connected with suffering and, what was more, apparently the author of it – or, at least, my bit! How could I say to people that there is a good God? He did not seem very good to me and, to make things far worse, it was not other people's suffering he might have caused; it was mine.

Was it really God who had made me like this? If they were to ask me how I felt about my bad vision, could I say that God does things like that? If they thought that I might go charging off into people's homes, portraying him in that fashion, they might think that I was likely to drive my new congregation away. They would not tolerate that and I would be out on my ear!

Suddenly, this all became a bit too personal and complicated. I resolved to bury my wondering as deeply as possible, just hoping it might never come to the surface again – not in the interviews, anyway.

It was over a year later, after many trials and many falls, that God caused me to fall down to my knees in front of him. I needed an encounter with him before I could discover his will for my life, my eyes and all that related to my creeping blindness. More of that in a moment.

The second area which needed my attention rose up and took over, almost as an anaesthetic to the first. I had long ago lost the ability to read anything but the largest print, so the Bible was a mass of greyish dots to me. The prayer book in common use at my church looked to be the same unintelligible nonsense, so how was I to take a church service? I supposed the answer would be to learn it all off by heart. That solution would have to suffice for the interviews.

Walking down the street without sighted assistance or without a guide dog was still a relatively safe activity for me in those days, but there was no way to read the house numbers on distant gateways or doorposts, so visiting was going to be tough.

Various visits to partially sighted and blind clergy around the country did very little to boost my confidence, but it did present some reassurances that I could give to the Board of Interview. If others could find a way, then surely I could. At least, I could show that I had tried to be practical.

The following summer, I packed a bag and set off, in fear and trembling, for the final grilling. A two-year process was coming to an end; I was on the way. After supper on the first evening of the national interviews I met for coffee with three of the ten candidates, vowing to keep as quiet as possible. I wanted to see which way the flow was going to go, before being public with any views or thoughts about anything. There was going to be no slipping up at the last hurdle!

The first one said, "I'm a travelling salesman, in ladies' garments. I don't really care whether they accept me or not, because I still have my old job, which I enjoy. I'm going to be pretty laid back about all this."

The second one said, "I want to save people from hellfire and damnation, but only those earning less than fifty thousand a year. The others will all be lost, anyway."

The third one said, "I've come because I speak the Welsh language and my Bishop says he needs more of us in the Church in Wales."

Suddenly, my own motives did not seem quite so awful after all. In fact, I began to feel that I would be far more acceptable to any sensible interviewer than these three. The longer I thought about it, the safer I felt. Self-righteousness produces a great sense of false security. I could almost hear myself thinking, "God, I thank you that I'm not like other men – robbers, evildoers, adulterers – or even like this tax collector. Or to be more precise, this travelling salesman."

The leaders called for volunteers to read at the church services. I hid at the back, my mouth firmly closed, trying not to be too noticeable. Demonstrating my inability to read in public would be a black mark against me, I imagined.

The remainder of those three days was a blur

of ineptitude, inadequate answering, and interview questioning which was often worse than the answers.

They asked me to chair a meeting consisting of all the other candidates – as a test of my chairmanship skills, presumably. The subject they asked me to introduce and discuss was "litter". I was appalled. I sat there, seething! What about the need to spread the gospel? What about the pastoral care needs of a parish? At a push, I could even have accepted a discussion on fundraising for the church; but *litter*? I couldn't believe it!

"Oh well," I remarked to Ginnie, as she drove me home, "I suppose the end justifies the means." I was completely sure of things to come. I knew I would pass the test; I knew I would be ordained, and that the next few years were organized. For the first time in many a year, I felt secure.

Life would be a winning streak after all. There would be a set of buffers up along the track somewhere, but for now I was safe from crashing. Now there would be an escape route, should it be needed.

As my sight continued to deteriorate, so grew the certainty that the company would have to let me go sooner rather than later. Here was my get-out. All that was needed now was a list of instructions about the theological training course and my new life could begin.

Following the rejection letter, self-pity came in like a tidal wave. What was wrong with me? Was I being punished for something? If I were being punished, then had I not struggled enough? Was there going to be no end; was there no plan I could make that would secure life for me?

Moving from being fully sighted to being blind in a process that takes many years doesn't feel particularly life threatening. I was well used to the decline. In itself, it would not be the end of the world. The cliff edge in my life was not the blindness per se. It was an insecurity of gigantic proportions with respect to finance and a concern that I would fall hundreds of feet onto the jagged rocks of financial ruin.

Without failing sight, my future would carry on, just like anyone else's. But potential financial loss and my own lack of self-worth threatened to drag me and the three people I loved down into a pit of despair. How could I secure a home for Ginnie? The expense of running our home and a car, let alone a family, was beyond her teacher's salary on its own. With the best will in the world, she would not cope financially without some input from my own gainful employment.

Our sons James and Robert would need help once they left school, and they wanted university education. Everything a man seeks to do for those he loves was being tugged away from me by events over which I had no control. The mists of uncertainty swirled around, provoking pressures behind the eyes and infiltrating my emotions before bursting out in fits of tears, bad humour and intolerance.

Autumn continued into winter. The days shortened. The longer the darkness outside, the deeper grew the darkness inside. I felt that a trap had been set for me by fate, and the gate had slammed shut. Plonked down on the path, among Ginnie's garden tubs – that was the only place for me to be. They had been so full of summer promise and now, as autumn came to an end, the plants were wilting and dying back, losing all their glory; dry twigs in the dripping rain. I felt quite at home with them. We had much in common with one another.

Rejection came up in unrelenting waves, and I was just getting nowhere. In fact, I was right back again at the beginning, with nowhere to go. It had taken me thirty years or so to reach a point of family security, but here I was, right back at the start line again.

"God, where are you, for heaven's sake?" That was my only prayer.

Now was the time to check that the lifesaver was there, ready and waiting to catch me. Having reached the point of bewildered despair, the events of the following twenty-four hours were to prove the truth of this text in the most practical and unexpected of ways:

There is no-one like the God of Jeshurun, who rides on the heavens to help you and on the clouds in his majesty. The eternal God is your refuge, and underneath are the everlasting arms.

DEUTERONOMY 33:26–27A

Encroaching blindness was leading me straight into the everlasting arms. One Sunday morning the week before Christmas, so many years ago that I lose track, we went to worship in a local church (not our own), and the sermon lives on as one of the key turning-points in my life.

The vicar, who later became a dear friend to me, said this at the end of his sermon: "Just as Jesus was born at Christmas all those centuries ago, so it is my prayer that one of you be born again this Christmastide."

Why was he talking at me? I could not see the pulpit, let alone the preacher, so for all I knew he could have been addressing some other individual altogether or, most likely, the whole congregation. Anyway, I took it personally. It felt like he had thrown a spear from his lofty place and it had landed in my chest. How personal! How ridiculous! The remark could not have been meant for me; I didn't even know the man. And what, I asked myself, was all that stuff about being "born again"?

As Christmas Eve Midnight Mass began a few days later, I started to pray. My prayer lasted for most of the service, beginning with the offering of such thoughts as, "Look, I've managed and organized my life pretty well, up until now. Nice house, nice car, nice kids, nice wife. I've got on well at work too; no one gets as far as I have without being able to see properly."

The self-congratulation stuff went on for a while, but then it really hit me again that I had reached the blocked end of the street. Without someone else's help – someone who could control and manage things better than myself – I could run off the edge of a cliff without noticing the impending disaster. If I lost my career, then I might just lose all the rest!

Something had to change. Something was going to give at any moment. By now, the begging accelerator foot was flat on the floor, and the prayer engine was revving uncontrollably. I begged and begged God Almighty to take the management load from my shoulders, the responsibility for my own life, and to change things to fit his planning and not mine.

The more I knew in the bottom of my heart that I would not be able to cope in the future, that things could only get worse, the more desperate the prayer became. The emotions related to the need to have someone else come and take over were palpable and my chest felt like it was seeking to contain a nuclear chain reaction.

God answered in a way which changed everything for me – literally everything. The time for going up to the altar rail to receive the Eucharist had come. To my annoyance, I had to break away from prayer and march up the aisle in a haze of boozy fumes coming from the man in front of me.

I had almost lost the mood completely by the time I got there. The new sanctuary lights were very bright and I was like a rabbit being blinded by the glare of car headlights. The struggle not to bump into anyone, coupled with the smell from Mr Best Bitter in front, took away from me the prayer spirit I had been in.

The moment seemed to have gone. The bread came by, and the wine. Then it was time to start back down through the dazzling glare of the sanctuary searchlights.

In the moment I began to push up with my hands on the altar rail, a man came and stood in front of me, threw his arms around my upper arms and back and lifted me about three inches off the ground – or so I remember it. Before he took hold of me, I did not have to open my eyes to know that he was there. I could feel him there.

This is not quite as strange a sensation as it may seem because, even by then, I was learning to feel the presence of lamp-posts and walls in the street before I smacked into them. It's a blind person's personal echo-location system. Using that sense, I simply did not have to open my eyes to know that he was there. At any rate, people do not hug other people without their knowing it!

Eventually he lowered me to the floor again and I immediately got my eyes open, but there was no one around! The priests were down at the other end, ministering to the long line of flock, and it could not have been one of them anyway, because they were too far away and they had their hands full with the administration of the sacrament.

Back in the pews, the next hymn had started. Ginnie turned to me. "What's the matter, darling?" I shook my head to indicate that everything was OK, but a dam had broken inside. The tears that rolled down my face – the reason for her question – did not stop for the next seven days. God had come to take things over.

The relief was overwhelming. The knowledge that God had come for me was certain and unmistakable. I had been given a new start in life. I had been born again.

Within what seems like no time at all, I had a dream. Without so much as a "by your leave", this set the scene for the rest of my life. I saw myself walking barefoot along a stony path which lay across the face of a rolling, heather-strewn mountain. I could even hear a curlew call on the distant hillside, giving out a mournful cry which so poignantly reflected the loneliness of my journey to that point.

The heather was in flower, the blueberries were bright blue, and the bees were busy in the sunshine with the clover. Not a single cloud whitened the deep blue above me, and a soft breeze was ruffling my hair.

At right angles to my path, ahead of me, was another track, coming down from the hilltop to my left, towards the valley floor. There, on his way down, the lonesome figure of Jesus himself slowly walked.

He was dressed in a long white robe, as one would expect, but his bare feet were cut to ribbons by the jagged edges of the ground he walked on. When I glanced down, so were mine. The soles were bruised, scratched and grazed, aching with tiredness, and the ankles were puffed up, like potatoes.

Straight away, we had something in common: feet which were cut and bruised from walking through the world. He had endured the effects of human life and so had I.

"This is wonderful," I thought. "Here, at last, is someone to talk to. Someone who will really understand; someone with all the time in the world to listen."

A nearby spreading thorn tree, just below where the two paths met, cast a shadow large enough to sit under, and to provide shelter from the heat of the day. There he soon stopped and beckoned for me to join him.

No words passed between us: I just sat beside him, a little to his right and a little behind. Over his shoulder, I could see what he was seeing. I remember being so thankful that bad eyesight never prevents people from looking with spiritual eyes, or feeling atmospheres with spiritual senses.

I wanted to comment on the fact that we shared bruised feet, in the hope that he might heal the soreness, but no words came. I wanted to ask him to touch my eyes with his finger, but suddenly it just did not seem important any more. Jesus seemed lost in his own thoughts; not concerned with my affairs, but with those of others in the villages in the valley below and on the opposite hillsides. This was not the time to talk.

My bleeding bare feet lay pointing up to the sky, about six inches from his right hand. He would only have to stretch a little forward, and my struggling walk through life would be so much easier. I willed and ached for him to do it, but he would not move. Then again, his feet were damaged, too, and I was not about to offer to heal them for him, either! Perhaps damaged feet were a gift to me, so that I could share just a little in his pain? Perhaps not.

When I began to see what he was looking at, I discovered with quite a shock that my feet, and their little difficulties, had gone out of focus. Try as I might, I couldn't concentrate on them. They did not seem important any more.

As his gaze moved slowly back and forth along the line of blue and grey hills, my eyes followed the movement of his head, and all I could see was pain.

Standing, staring up at us, were grieving widows, failing husbands and wounded children.

There were so many people whose illnesses were the real kings of their lives, ruling over everything and destroying the peace in their souls. There was anger and frustration, depression and unhappiness. There was anxiety and unfulfilment. There were hearts with little vacuums in them, longing to be filled with something permanent – but searching fruitlessly.

There was arthritis and cancer and bent and broken bones, sufferers of diseases of all kinds longing for help. I suppose there must have been happy people as well – it is just that I did not notice them. The broken ones were much easier to see, for some reason. They stood out from the crowd, and were in the majority.

If I could have seen Jesus' face at that moment, I am sure I would have seen him crying. I looked towards the valley towns, with the vision or perspective that an eagle might have, and saw the worst thing of all – mothers holding dead babies in their arms, so shocked in the midst of their own pain that they could not find the emotion to respond to the horror of their situations.

Whether or not Jesus was crying, I will never know, but I certainly did.

Such a sight of horror was too much to bear. These were the words that sprang to mind, as the centre of my concentration lifted from my aching feet to the aching world. The words were the sounds from the lips of those fathers and mothers and children below me. They had raised their faces towards our hillside position, caught sight of Jesus and were encouraging each other:

> *Lift up your eyes to the heavens, look at the earth*
> *beneath; the heavens will vanish like smoke,*
> *the earth will wear out like a garment and its*
> *inhabitants die like flies. But my salvation will*
> *last forever, my righteousness will never fail.*

ISAIAH 51:6

"Send me down to the valley, Lord," I whispered into his ear, "and let me help them."

The practical outworking of that dream was yet to be revealed, but for now it was closing with a warm glow.

Into my life they began to come in a steady stream.

Beautiful people who should be flowering for Christ, and yet were flattened by sickness and injury and by the aftermath of miscarriages, abortions, stillborn children, cot deaths and teenage suicide.

I lost sight of my own "torn feet", my blindness. God was doing something for me by replacing my sorrows with his sorrows; the pain I felt for me with his pain for them. He was exchanging their hurts for his healing love; their deaths for his salvation; their sorrows for his joys; their griefs for his peace. His healing grace releases all these things, and what joy it is, through Christ's tears, to watch the flowers of his kingdom grow and blossom, to his glory.

As I reflected on the question that had echoed out from the audience member at the close of the meeting which starts this book, I didn't tell my waiting audience any of my dream. Instead I told them the story I've already told you about the twenty-three-year-old girl who had come to a meeting, stumbling and dragging one foot along the floor, face and body misshapen by a birth defect. I talked of her healing and the loss of it. I spoke of not questioning her judgment with my own thoughts and ideas. So I had blessed her and let her go.

I stopped at the end of the story and looked in the direction of the questioner and raised my eyebrows as if to enquire about the sufficiency of my response. There was silence. No answer I have is ever good enough to satisfy.

I pushed on quickly to other things. There were more people queuing for ministry and there was kingdom work to do.

"Thank you, Lord, that you use such strange circumstances to work your purposes," I prayed as I stepped down and back into the ministry melee. "Thank you that you have brought me to this place in my life and thank you for all the stepping stones along the way that have led us to this most joyful and miraculous point."

What stepping stones? Where would they all lead? What miraculous interventions were waiting along the way?

CHAPTER 4
Into The Well

I bumped into the vicar of a nearby church in a crowded shopping centre. He was wandering around among the disinterested shoppers, asking people if they knew the way to his church. He turned to speak to me. But as he recognized me he became quite emotional and didn't greet me in the friendly way he normally did.

Why was he asking for directions to his own church? What had happened to him? Here is the story.

A young and attractive couple stood on the vicarage doorstep, politely requesting that they be given a guided tour around the ancient and picturesque Norman church across the road. My friend, the vicar in charge, duly complied.

One set of their grandparents had been married there seventy-five years before. They were visiting the area and checking up on their family roots. At the end of their guided tour, punctuated by many gasps of delighted surprise and wide-eyed amazement at the beauty and antiquity of the structure, furnishings and contents, they asked:

"How many years ago did they last have a Sunday morning church service in here?"

Their words had wrapped around him and enveloped him like a great grey raincloud. A tidal wave of depression flooded over my clergy friend as the realization dawned. His visitors (perhaps like many others) were innocently assuming that his church was a religious museum, his guided tour a glimpse into a bygone age of an outdated spirituality, and he himself no more than the curator of a fine and ancient example of English architecture.

Eventually, the visiting couple left, nonchalantly tossing a few coins on to a brass plate by the door, thanking my friend profusely for his time, commending him for his obvious caring for the old place.

Closing the heavy doors behind his visitors, as hand in hand they skipped and chattered their way down the sunlit path to the churchyard gate and the main road, my friend returned to his altar. There he prostrated himself on the ground before it, crying out for forgiveness, direction and grace.

Was he, he wondered in prayer, overreacting or had he caught the faintest glimpse of something very painful and disturbing to Christ himself? Returning home, he exchanged his clerical collar for an open-neck casual shirt, and wandered down to, and around, the nearby shopping centre for almost an hour. He occasionally asked the busy passers-by for directions to his own church.

No one could help him. No one knew where it was.

Sometimes his question provoked a "Oh my God!" or "God help us!" or "Jesus Christ!" But he recognized these outbursts for what they were. Poor, shrivelled and crippled ends of prayer, lost behind the blasphemies of those who seemed to know nothing of the reality of God.

Interestingly, he noticed that for some reason, they still appeared to find a need to speak of God, even if it was only through their clenched teeth. They certainly did not know how to find his church. This gloomy picture began to feel even worse to him with the freshening realization, and a sharpening sense of responsibility to those around him, that God still wants to use his body, the church, to offer to the world a perfect moral and spiritual model.

Throughout all the many upheavals and changes of the past twenty centuries, his revelation of good news in Jesus Christ has been and still is the cause and source of passionate, self-giving love. So, are we, the church, only a museum, or are we holding something which is very precious: the gospel of Jesus' love?

After he encountered me, we retreated swiftly to a coffee shop to talk. We agreed with one another that this love, the true light offered to the world, had been seen in action in every age, and throughout the whole world; it could once again have a major impact on every nation, and in the middle of every political situation, as well as on all age groups, temperaments and conditions of people.

We reminded each other that the three years of our Saviour's ministry on earth did more to regenerate and soften the hearts of mankind than all the philosophical discourses and all the exhortations of our secular moralists put together! Had all that love and power evaporated? Can we still expect to find it at work even among our congregations?

That crowded afternoon in the shopping centre, my clergy colleague and I reached a sort of "Slough of Despond". A depressing weight had squeezed out of him all his enthusiasm for simply being the one who supervised and led the weekly rituals of church life.

From that day on, we knew that things had to change. There had to be more: there had to be a way for us to move on. There had to be a place outside the walls of the church building where God would be recognized for who he is. There had to be a place where theory would break through into reality and what many saw as just ecclesiastical rhetoric would become received, simple truth.

As we left the coffee shop and stood, slightly bewildered, among the milling shoppers, our hearts ached and cried out to move on. We knew there had to be more to this kingdom life than holding worship services for God but seeing few or no miracles. Could we begin to work with God, who actually does miracles to prove the truth of the message of the cross?

Gone was the desire to merely speak about a God who wants to change his parishioners' lives; now we longed to see those changes occur and needy souls helped.

Together we yearned for the cross of Christ to be

recognized in those streets, not only as the central symbol of Christian faith, but as a potent message of the working power of God. To hold out the healing light of Jesus Christ would mean reaching out.

We knew that the commonly accepted flow of church life around us would probably be in the opposite direction. The tendency of all religions is to care more for religion than for humanity. Jesus, though, cared more for humanity than he did for religion; his compassion for the needs of ordinary people seems to have been much more important to him than the customs and habits of the professionally religious people.

Standing in the swirling crowd, between the department stores, almost unaware of the shoppers, we went on talking. We became aware, as our conversation unfolded, that the natural instinct of contemporary Christianity, for a myriad of reasons, is to find ways to soften Jesus' radical teaching and let his compassionate vision for all these passing folk drift out of focus. Then the amazing message of Jesus no longer impacts our own lives or the lives of those we want to reach.

Then, for no obvious reason that I could tell, my friend's heart began to lift.

"We ought to know, against the flow of the world-view," he was reminding both of us, "that it is in Christ that the whole universal structure of things, including everything that goes on in the lives of all these people side-stepping around us in the street, holds together. Actually, a large proportion of those who walk past us every day have lives that are falling apart, or have fallen apart, and it seems to so many of them that there is nothing for them to do but live with it, without knowing the divine longing to piece them back together again."

He flicked a small Bible out of his pocket and began to read to me:

> *For by him all things were created: things in heaven and on earth, visible and invisible, whether thrones or powers or rulers or authorities; all things were created by him and for him. He is before all things, and in him all things hold together.*
>
> COLOSSIANS 1:16–17

Around us is so much that is in need of new life. My friend was feeling, with a new and almost bold frustration, that the kingdom of God is full of the power that raised Jesus from the dead. Those of us who have begun to live in this kingdom dynamic know, as a direct consequence, that we are living in our Father's world. We know that it is a big and healing kingdom and that perhaps we have begun to explore only a tiny part of it.

As long as we keep the word of God and its author as our foundation and base camp, there is much exploring to do. This world of Christian healing has wide and distant horizons towards which we must travel, and some of them are still unfamiliar. But it is his kingdom – all of it.

Around this time there were three of us together in a small prayer group, meeting once a week and praying for any sick people we knew. And now we had reached a crossroads. How could we break out of secluded prayer, and into face-to-face care, prayer and healing like the apostles did?

This became a huge issue with the three of us, but our own church was not one to let lay people, with no ecclesiastical authority to minister, have opportunities to explore the idea of the priesthood of all believers.

As a prayer group, we had been relegated to the damp, freezing, tiny room at the rear of the church hall, which had been serving as a junk-room for many years and a happy hunting-ground for the local mice and woodworm. Little did anyone else know how that awful dank room glowed with the light of Christ, as we prayed with him.

Holy frustration at such restricting circumstances and lack of acceptance built and built. Requests for God to use us more openly and freely crept into every prayer evening. By the onset of our last winter in the little room at the back of the church hall, nothing seemed to be growing and we were miserable! What could we do about space?

One local parish minister took pity on us, offering us the use of his church hall for two evenings a week in exchange for a small financial retainer. We enjoyed the increased space to move in. There were plenty of chairs to sit on, and no carpet to be stained with spots of anointing oil. But there were two mighty disadvantages to our new home.

The facilities were abominable. There were no kitchen arrangements – just a power point for a kettle. The single outside lavatory would not have been out of place in a museum of nineteenth-century social history! The building was situated quite close to the nearby canal, now largely disused, and the village river-rats took it upon themselves to nest under the floorboards. Hopefully, there was enough worship going on to cover their scratching, but the quiet moments were a different kettle of fish altogether.

There were many times when startled visitors had to be quickly reassured that the noises were only birds building their nests in the eaves! In the end, we had to move our meetings to the rooms adjoining the local Methodist church, which the minister had graciously allowed us to borrow – but only for a short while.

Here we met Postman Pat. This colourful chap was a large transfer, stuck on the window of the church children's playroom – the room we used for our healing services. The heat of the summer sun, pouring through the glass, had melted his face, collapsing the whole of the front of his head down on to neck and chest. Hardly a picture of Christian healing! We cunningly arranged the chairs for our services so that everyone had their backs to poor Postman Pat, who, we hoped, would not suffer too much from this rejection in his hour of need! But at least there were no rats.

Operating in a cross-denominational context is never easy. We began to hunt seriously for a place of our own. Those were happy times, though. We were roughing it for the Lord and we really did not mind one bit. To look back at our two homes – one shared with the canal rats and the other with Postman Pat – is to see those days through rose-tinted spectacles, the rose colouring being provided by the answers to prayer that filled our lives to the "overflow pipe".

Suddenly, one, two and then three local clergy began to take an interest in our tiny group's prayer life, in a way that was so new and reassuring. Through the things they commented on, it seemed that they actually thought we were an OK bunch of folks after all!

One of these clergymen came to our home, and was nothing short of thrilled by my stories of the outworking of God's grace, and how much we were becoming dedicated to prayer, and the idea of ministry to others. During this conversation, I plucked up the courage to say, "One day, we could have our own place, a place dedicated to Jesus; just a place for him to do what he wants to do – anything he likes, as long as it improves life for people who know that they need him."

"That'll take five years at least to get going," came the reply from this short and stocky vicar, lost in a pile of sofa cushions. "But don't give up; just keep praying for it, and if God wants to give it to you, he will." When he left the house, I got down to a bit of serious talking to God who, after all, owns the cattle on a thousand hills. Someone had once said to me, "If you roll up your sleeves with God, he will roll them up with you." That was what I wanted to do.

"There's a place in your heart for us somewhere! You know where it is, and if you want us to have it, then please start preparing it." I talked to him about this "five years" business. I felt him telling me that it would take three, and I had no reason to doubt him. This is the God who outstrips our expectations over so many things; why not over this issue?

I typed out this promise on a card, stapling it to the rim of the pocket inside the lid of my briefcase, so that I would be reminded of it every day. Every morning as I sat at my office desk in the factory and opened the lid, there it was, his promise to me, and I could begin each day by giving thanks for it.

The card read: "I covenant with the Lord God Almighty that I will serve him and worship him in a dedicated healing centre in three years." In the bottom right-hand corner, I wrote the date: "March 1st 1990."

As the dreadful storm-clouds of redundancy threatened yet again, for the third time in three years, I reached the end of the trail. Ginnie was in full agreement. She had watched me slipping and sliding down the slope of despair, desperately hanging on to my job with a growing tenacity, increasingly swamped by the fear of an impending disaster as my sight went downhill and I could not cope with the work any longer. Surely, I would have to walk away from the factory life that had sustained us and our home for all those years.

Ginnie encouraged and supported me, on and on, until the Lord finally showed his hand. Towards the end of our time at the Methodist church, a local lad came to one of our open evenings, and mentioned that an old chapel in the town had a "For Sale" sign over the door. It had been empty for a number of years, and was nearly derelict, but he thought it might make a good healing centre.

We went, we saw the ruined state of it; and we lost courage. But God seemed to have left it there just for us, so we set about the legal wrangling to acquire it. My heart was not exactly leaping for joy at this point. We were about to exchange scratching rats and dripping postmen for spiders, broken windows and rotten floorboards. Would all this ever come right?

But at least the old chapel had all the potential we needed. A large main room would do well enough for conferences and healing services, and the side rooms were sufficient to provide two quiet ministry rooms, and an office for administration.

Across the back of the building there were gents' and ladies' toilets, a boiler room large enough to double as a storeroom and a kitchen which, given a lot of work, could be made large enough to eat in. Above all, it would be all ours. We would be free to come and go as we pleased, able to arrange for people to come by appointment, and no longer in competition with any other activity. It was filthy, but it was wonderful!

The card stapled into the briefcase lid had kept me going for those three years. It was bent and torn and grubby and, in the nick of time, a place had at last been found. My lovely heavenly Father was true to his word and I walked out of the factory gates for the last time.

On 1 March 1993, exactly three years to the day, just as he had promised, we opened the doors of The Well Centre and, at forty-eight years old, I left the factory behind for ever. A lady friend of Ginnie's presented me with a paperweight, as a sort of housewarming gift to sit on my new desk in my new office. On the top of it is inscribed:

You did not choose me, but I chose you and appointed you to go and bear fruit – fruit that will last. Then the Father will give you whatever you ask in my name.

JOHN 15:16

The great day had come. The Well Centre opened. I suppose we could have had a band, lots of flags and a press launch, but I could not remember Jesus' ministry beginning like that, so we didn't try. If this was to be the ministry of availability, then we would just sit, pray and wait.

My last few weeks in the factory had been largely absorbed in financial planning – and there was no way that we as a family were going to make it! I pored over the figures with a strong magnifying glass, until the tears came to my sore eyes, but I couldn't make any reasonable sense of them.

Everywhere I looked, the red outweighed the black. We had promised, and committed, resources which we simply would not have. I have never felt so downright irresponsible and vulnerable in my whole life. Waiting at home was an overbearing mortgage, gas and electricity bills, and two sons straining at the leash to get through university, which would be impossible without parental financial aid. Perhaps I was going crazy.

There were no guarantees here at all. I was committed to The Well, with no gainful employment, and consequently with no idea of what my income would be.

One thought kept pounding away in my head, drowning out the doubts and fears. Something good was going to happen – tomorrow. How that goodness would show itself, I did not appreciate at the time. I imagined that it would be something very healing: some vague but nevertheless real understanding that God was going to assure me of something very much better than I had ever had before.

But it was not just the financial concern which had to be surrendered to God. The frustration, the anxiety and the creeping sense of insecurity – all had to be offered up. At the peak of the emotional battle, God's words were quite clear:

"I want you to give up working for me, and start working with me."

Since those frightening days, I have discovered Hebrews 11:13, which illuminates this balance between the agony of indecision I was facing and the knowledge that there was so much to come. The writer of Hebrews had been talking about all those patriarchs who had gone forward into the unknown, for no other reason than that they knew by faith that they had to.

He writes that all these people were still living by faith when they died. They did not receive the things promised; they only saw them, and welcomed them from a distance. They admitted that they were aliens and strangers on earth. That particular extract from Hebrews goes on to discuss Moses in this light. He regarded disgrace for the sake of Christ (analogous, in my case, to holding the title "disabled") as of greater value than the treasures of Egypt, because he was looking ahead to his reward.

It was through his faith that he left Egypt, not fearing the king's anger. He persevered, because he saw him who is invisible.

This sort of person seemed to me to have had a transfigured perspective on life. All things seem to have been just a part of their walk with God, towards some unseen and greater goal. Their eyes were up, and over the horizon.

The whole basis of my insecurity had been failing sight. Now I had reached the point of no return – when decisions were being made so fast, and there was no way back. I learned a whole new meaning of the psalm which says:

I lift up my eyes to the hills – where does my help come from? My help comes from the Lord, the Maker of heaven and earth.

PSALM 121:1–2

The idea that "lifting up" and "offering" might just be the same thing led me, for the first time, to the principle that I should offer my eyes – the source of all my conflicts – to God; and that he would, somehow, be able to use them. In the end, this was the only thing left for me to do. God was teaching me to trust him, the hard way.

The place we had named The Well was a mess. One of the trustees (Maris) had chosen the name to reflect the idea that the centre might be like the well where Jesus sat and spoke to the needy woman. She came to the well to slake her thirst, but as Jesus spoke to her, the wonderful offer of everlasting water was given, by him for all.

Even with this encouraging truth in mind, it was difficult to view the state of the building we had walked into with anything but dismay. Yet hard work and prayer would eventually see our hopes fulfilled as God blessed the work.

We started with rotten floorboards, peeling paintwork; broken windows, an antiquated central heating system that hardly worked and no telephone. There were no curtains at the windows, and the kitchen should have been put out of bounds, on health grounds.

The lavatories were old, cracked and rusty; the roof-tiles had slipped, were often broken and sometimes missing altogether. If the building looked like anything at all, in those early days, it certainly did not look like a peaceful place of healing! All the money we had was given to the solicitors to deal with the legalities. If the building was to be made habitable, then the work would have to be done by us. There were days and days of hard work ahead. We were dirty and broke!

"Oh Lord," I prayed, while digging out a floorboard which dry rot had almost disintegrated, "we came here to work with you, not to scrub floors and paintwork! What will we do after all this hard work, if no one comes near the place?"

The basic renovations and repairs were eventually completed. Happily, our plans for the various rooms came to fruition. What started as an office has since been reborn and is now a private prayer and ministry room. All the leaky holes in the roof were patched up, and the crumbling, falling, rain-drenched ceiling plaster was renewed.

The generosity of those who come to us now enables the upkeep of the building to be carried out by professionals, instead of our willing, sore and amateurish hands.

There are times when God's encouragement for the

work that any of us are engaged in seems to descend on us by the bucketful. A whole dollop was on its way, just when it was badly needed.

I was sitting at home one evening, cleaned up from yet another day's scraping and painting shortly after the opening of The Well, when the phone rang. It was a friend from the West Country who had not been in touch for some months.

It was good to hear her voice again. After the pleasantries, she said, "Mike, I'm not sure what's happening to you these days, but I have a bit of Scripture for you. May I read it over the phone?" It was from Isaiah, and it was just for me:

> ... *and if you spend yourselves on behalf of the hungry and satisfy the needs of the oppressed, then your light will rise in the darkness, and your night will become like the noonday. The Lord will guide you always; he will satisfy your needs in a sun-scorched land and will strengthen your frame. You will be like a well-watered garden, like a spring whose waters never fail. Your people will rebuild the ancient ruins and will raise up the age-old foundations; you will be called Repairer of Broken Walls, Restorer of Streets with Dwellings.*
>
> ISAIAH 58:10–12

God was listening to my every thought and accepting my

every offering. He was going to change us (or at least me, as the scripture was for me) from a place of struggling disability into a "well-watered garden" – which I later understood to be The Well.

What was more, my "night" (by which I assumed he meant my lack of vision) was to be made into a noonday, through what was going on. Amazing! I was over the moon. And the lovely folk who had opened the Centre with me – Ann, Maris, Sheila and Jean – would become known as rebuilders and restorers. That is healing and wholeness! The whole Well Centre plan was going to work!

"Now," my caller went on, before I had time to relate the story of the opening of The Well, "here is something else for you, as well. I don't know, but I think the Lord really wants you to have this gift – for yourself and for you alone."

She read from Proverbs that a generous man would prosper, and that he who refreshes others will himself be refreshed. That was the moment when all the strain of the private family financial worries flew out of the window, snuffed out by the sheer power of the word of God. Within six months my worrying mortgage was paid off completely, enough money was set aside to put both sons through university, and I had acquired a private income of about £1 a month more than I had been earning in industry. That's breathtaking!

More importantly, the people began to come. At first, they came into The Well in very small numbers, but the flow gradually increased, and there seemed no end to God's favour towards them. As people began to respond, I was reminded of Jesus' wonderful invitation:

> *Whoever is thirsty, let him come; and whoever wishes, let him take the free gift of the water of life.*
>
> REVELATION 22:17

There were many miracles to watch, and much to give thanks for. It was not that we saw hundreds of people getting up out of wheelchairs or throwing off medically incurable diseases. We saw our small share of such things, but the real miracles came in the strengthening, the rebuilding, the refurbishing, the mending of broken lives to make whole people again – or as whole as we can be in a fallen world.

Of course, all that was to change. Events were to overtake us, God would take a hand in our teaching and, joy upon joy, he would soon begin to glorify his name through miracle after miracle in the healing of the sick and the injured.

Although our eyes had been opened wide by all the teachings we had received over the years, it was God's grace which made things happen.

Solicitors, doctors and drug addicts, airline pilots and single mothers, clergy and housewives; God does not mind who they are, or where they come from. And what were they bringing with them into The Well in those early days? Just about anything that it is possible to imagine: from abuse to ME; from sexual difficulties of all kinds to physical ailments; from mental illness to marriage strains. God was touching all of them.

Here is a report from those early days, given in his church by a thrilled husband about his thrilled wife! This is Margaret's story:

If Margaret (my wife) were here today I know she would be standing here instead of me. As it is she is sunning herself in Australia for a few weeks. Some 15 years ago, when we were living in Hong Kong, Margaret visited Water World, a theme park. She was sitting in a big rubber ring and gently gliding down waterslides between small pools. As Margaret was in one of these small pools, a group of lads came down the waterslide behind her in tandem and crashed into her.

She was catapulted forward and banged her head on the bottom of the pool, as the ring she was on rotated forwards. The Park would normally have had someone stationed at the top of the slide to prevent this happening, but on this occasion they did not.

It took a number of weeks for the extent of the injury to become apparent. In essence there was severe whiplash damage to the neck. Over the intervening years the neck did not heal. Despite

*very extensive medical investigation and treatment
the injury proved impossible to cure. The best that
could be achieved was palliative care for the reduced
mobility, pain, nausea and headaches. In the mid
1990s Margaret also developed a frozen shoulder.
This compounded the difficulties because pain in
one part of her upper body meant overcompensation
from another part, which in turn became the next
problem to be treated.*

*Margaret did receive healing in October 1999,
which increased the movement in her neck and
shoulder and enabled her to travel to London for a
few days to receive treatment at a frozen shoulder
clinic. For many years Margaret could not shop
by herself, as she couldn't lift very much and was
generally very restricted in terms of what she could do.*

*She had to plan her route in the car as she
couldn't make left turns without feeling nauseous. In
an average week she would visit the physiotherapist
at least once and often more. The physiotherapist
believes that Margaret had irreversible neuro-tissue
damage, for which the only treatment was palliative.*

*She went from one mini-crisis to the next.
Margaret's condition would be something she would
have to live with. There would be trips to the
chiropractor or osteopath whenever her neck was
out of alignment (leading to severe headaches and
nausea), and regular trips to other therapists*

as the need arose.

She would often have to retreat to bed to lie down to relieve the pain and nausea. Her quality of life was severely impaired as there was so much she couldn't do and with which she needed help. The prospect of how she would be in later years frankly frightened her.

When Mike Endicott came in November for the healing weekend workshop and service, Margaret and I were privileged and very blessed to host him. From the moment he walked through our door we both sensed that here was someone special and extraordinary.

Margaret's neck began easing almost immediately. It was an amazing experience just having some time with them as we talked about all sorts of things, but mainly about Mike's healing ministry and how the weekend was going. The miraculous seemed to be at the heart of so much of what Mike did in his ministry. Can the miraculous ever be commonplace?

On Sunday after the service Margaret went to Mike for healing ministry and I also joined them. Mike took Margaret's hands in his and asked if she really believed she would be healed? She affirmed that she did. Mike asked some questions about the accident that led to the injury and asked whether Margaret had ever forgiven the lads who caused the injury? She hadn't really thought about forgiving the

*lads and maybe didn't even think to blame them.
However, she said she forgave them (and really
meant it) and then slumped backwards and had to
be supported.*

*Mike thanked and praised Jesus for a period of
time. Margaret remembers she felt little after she
forgave the lads. As Mike was praying she felt the
bones and muscles moving in her neck, back and
shoulders and she seemed to grow taller as her neck
straightened.*

*Margaret had been completely healed and made
whole by the Lord Jesus.*

*Both our lives were transformed that weekend
and will never be the same again. Margaret can now
do things she hasn't been able to do for over 15 years
and remains completely healed to this day. Thank
you Jesus!*

*Jesus taught that the kingdom of God is near. On
that Sunday last November the kingdom was here
in this church. All we have to do is reach out and
embrace what Jesus dearly wants all of us to have, a
life in his kingdom.*

*O Lord, you are my God; I will exalt you and
praise your name, for in perfect faithfulness you
have done marvellous things, things planned long
ago (Isaiah 25:1).*

PHIL

As The Well became a more accepted part of church life in this part of the world, so the longing began to deepen in me that we should be under properly authorized church leadership. But how could this be?

CHAPTER 5
Thinking the Unthinkable

The time had come around again to see the Bishop. It was always a pleasure to turn up on his doorstep, drink a cup of his coffee and keep him informed of all that was taking place at The Well.

I went every six months or so and on this particular occasion I was comfortably at home in the rocking-chair in his office. My guide dog, Yates, was lying at my feet and keeping a watchful eye on the coffee table because of the plate of biscuits that, in his view, dominated it!

We talked a while. The Bishop spoke of Jesus with a love that was obvious. He always encouraged me and he assured me that our three years of work at The Well had been healthy and purposeful.

I sipped my coffee and waited to raise the subject that was at the top of my agenda. I wanted to enlist his help in the search for a clergy person to head up the team and the ministry. It was a sensible next step, would secure our credibility and ensure that there was a daily working oversight of both the Centre and our burgeoning healing theology.

We were trying to grasp the nettle and deal with a difficult problem. The Well Centre was thriving but it was a stand-alone operation. It was not an outreach project of a church; it was not even an activity going on in a church building. It was not demonstrably under the authority of the church and we believed it should be.

I felt secure in the knowledge that Christ is the head of the body, and we were a part of it. But I felt a little uneasy because we were unable to demonstrate to other Christians that we were not "unguided missiles", out of control and prone to error.

We were determined to find a member of the clergy to head up the team. The Trustees could not afford to offer a salary but we had taken financial risks before. We could not have found him or her a house to live in either but believed the Lord would provide.

Armed with a mandate from the Trustees, I began to look around. I made lists of retired pastors but they had all really retired! I made lists of the ones with no money but they were too poor to come. We advertised in the church press to no avail.

What was God doing? I could only conclude that he was making me wait for the right person to become available. Then, one late summer evening, walking home from The Well, I knocked again on the gates of heaven:

"Lord, show me the man! Help me to see the one you've chosen for us!"

I knew immediately in the deep reaches of my being, that a provision had been made by God; a clergyman would be provided. It was probably just my lack of vision that prevented me from coming across God's choice. What had I missed? Where else was there to look?

Towards the end of our time together, I was on the point of broaching the subject when the Bishop shook me rigid with the question:

"Would you like me to ordain you?"

My mind went into a spin. Where did that come from? I remember feeling so grateful that the rocking-chair had arms, because without them I would have fallen off!

"You can't just do that!" I blurted out.

"There may be a way," he responded.

"But, I'm too old!"

"I know how old you are."

"I can't see well enough to study, I'm blind! I don't want to leave my work and go to theological college for three years." I was fighting the logic of the idea but the Bishop was dismantling my arguments as quickly as I raised them.

"I don't want you to," he countered.

In a final attempt to conclude the conversation, I played my trump card: "But I don't want to go through that selection process. I did it years ago and got rejected. It was awful!"

He had his answer to that one, too. "I've just selected you."

He finished our talk by adding, "Ordination won't open many doors for you, but it will certainly oil the hinges!"

Shortly afterwards I found myself outside in the sunshine, having departed with a vague remark about needing to pray about it. "Perhaps we could meet again soon and discuss it further," I had said.

It had not dawned on any of us that God's answer lay, as it so often does, right under our noses. This would take some thinking about. I went home to tell Ginnie what the Bishop had said. She sat me down on the garden seat outside the back door with another mug of coffee and left me to start thinking it all through.

Now was the time to reflect upon what ordination might mean. I hadn't seriously considered these things before, as I had previously offered myself for selection for other and far more dubious motives. It seemed to be a door that it wasn't right to push, according to my old thinking.

These verses came straight into my mind:

> ... now that you have tasted that the Lord is good. As you come to him, the living Stone – rejected by men but chosen by God and precious to him – you also, like living stones, are being built into a spiritual house to be a holy priesthood, offering spiritual sacrifices acceptable to God through Jesus Christ.
>
> 1 PETER 2:3–5

Reading that scripture again, it seemed to me that the idea of a "royal priesthood" was addressed not just to the leaders of the congregations, but also to the congregations themselves.

Should not Christian priesthood be a function of the faith community as a whole? I could not find anywhere in the New Testament where any individual Christian is described as a "priest". Jesus Christ himself is the great High Priest; and nowhere is the term "priesthood" applied to a special group within the church.

The whole community of saints seemed to me to be "priestly" in character, by virtue of the relationship of Jesus to his body, his people. This notion of priesthood has always been basic to my understanding of the church, and I take it to be true to the teaching of the New Testament.

I had often heard this doctrine referred to as "the priesthood of all believers", but perhaps that term fails to encompass the New Testament concept adequately. Some people seem to associate the idea with their right to vote at church meetings. In some denominations, it would appear that the idea was lost altogether in the setting up of a special professional group in the church.

Did my Bishop want me to join some special elite group who alone were entrusted with the power of God? Surely not. The New Testament speaks of Christians, those for whom Jesus the Lamb of God was slain, in these terms:

You have made them to be a kingdom and priests
to serve our God, and they will reign on the earth.

REVELATION 5:10

This was a word from God for all – not just leaders or
ordained ministers.

It seemed to me that the understanding of "priesthood"
clearly conveyed by the New Testament is not that every
person can be his or her own "priest". Nor is it saying
that each Christian must be a "priest" to his or her fellow
Christians, though the requirement for mutual service and
self-giving love in the body of Christ is important for us
to grasp.

I gradually began to understand more clearly that
each believer somehow shares in the priestly activity which
is characteristic of the church as a whole. Looking at this
from a different point of view altogether, I remembered
that bishops or "overseers" were a vital element of the
structure of the early church. The office of elder, presbyter
or church leader evolved into the "clergy" we discover in
later periods of church history.

As all these reflections, prompted by the Bishop's
words, went on in my mind, another jigsaw piece was
struggling to drop into my outstretched hands and be
fitted into my mental map. It occurred to me that in this
matter of ordination, individualism may be foreign to the
spirit of the Bible.

Certainly, we do not need a human priest to act as an

intermediary between us and Christ for our salvation or for our continuing growth in the Christian faith and life. Christ is our mediator, and we have access to his throne of grace and mercy:

> *Who is he that condemns? Christ Jesus, who died*
> *– more than that, who was raised to life – is at the*
> *right hand of God and is also interceding for us.*
>
> ROMANS 8:34

> *For there is one God and one mediator between*
> *God and men, the man Christ Jesus…*
>
> 1 TIMOTHY 2:5

When I came to Christ as an individual, I felt incorporated into his body, not as an isolated unit, but as one of a group of people. The stress here ought to be on our interdependence, not our independence.

The Well had to become an integral part of the body, part of this royal priesthood. We wanted to offer spiritual sacrifices acceptable to God through Jesus Christ. This is what the Scriptures call us to do:

> *Therefore, I urge you, brothers, in view of God's*
> *mercy, to offer your bodies as living sacrifices, holy*
> *and pleasing to God – this is your spiritual act of*
> *worship. Do not conform any longer to the pattern*
> *of this world, but be transformed by the renewing*

*of your mind. Then you will be able to test and
approve what God's will is – his good, pleasing
and perfect will.*

ROMANS 12:1–2

But what does it mean? What does this holy Christian priesthood, formed by all of us together in the church, actually do? These were the questions that came to me next. What are these sacrifices that Peter tells us we should be offering through Jesus Christ?

In Revelation 8:3 the saints, the holy ones, are offering up their prayers. Another angel who had a golden censer came and stood at the altar. He was given much incense to offer, with the prayers of all the saints, on the golden altar before the throne.

The sacrificial prayers of Christians are heard in heaven and make a difference!

With such sacrifices of praise God is well pleased. In ancient Israel the sacrificial system, given by God under the old covenant, prefigured the new covenant, under which Jesus himself was the one, full, perfect and sufficient sacrifice for sin. Offering our sacrifice of praise includes giving him all that we are and everything we do, in love and obedience.

These somewhat convoluted thought patterns were to serve me well later when teaching about the corporate holiness of the church; understanding the reality of it was another important piece of the jigsaw. Above all, it became clear to me that it is the whole body that Christ is calling to shine, not just its leaders.

So, was I being called to be a clergyman? Not if it just meant being licensed to bury the dead and take church services. Are our clergy intended to be merely decorative? I could not stand being that. I wanted to be in my jeans, on my knees before the throne of grace, up to my eyeballs with ministering to people who were in pain. That was where I felt at home. That was my calling.

By now I had discovered that the gifts of the Holy Spirit are wonderful and are such a vibrant witness to the presence of the living God. But I knew that the greatest gift I could ever have would be that of bringing others into the divine presence. After that, what happens is between God and the sufferer. I was ready to be an "overseer" if we were all going to be in the "priesthood" together.

By the time my next six-monthly trip to the Bishop's house came around again I had studied, mentally fought over, argued about, and tried to rationally discuss many aspects of ordination in the Anglican Church. I had concluded that it would give the team at The Well the one thing we had wanted and felt was appropriate: it would place us under proper spiritual authority.

As a small piece of my preparation for that day, I contacted a number of clergymen around the country, asking them the same question: What does ordination mean to you?

The answers were various, and this variety did not

really help at all. On the one hand I was told: "Just go out and have a few beers the night before. Enjoy it!" From the other end of the spectrum came one statement which startled me: "Ordination will make you holy."

Did this mean something would change? Hurriedly I asked the gentleman, "How do you define holiness?"

"A holy person is someone who is set aside for God," he responded.

That could mean anything. Putting down the phone, I sighed, collapsing back into my chair.

Would ordination simply make me a full-time church official? Was that all it would be? There had to be more. I did not know it then, but that conversation was to switch on a new light, an enormous desire to seek the meaning in my own life of the word "holy" and to search for it for myself. In the end, I saw something through all this that comes a little later – that being set aside for God must surely have a great deal to do with imitating him, especially in the way he did healing ministry.

We had searched for an authorized leader, and God was going to give us one.

The day originally chosen for my ordination was the same date as that set for the first ordinations of women in Wales to the priesthood, so I had opted out and persuaded the Bishop to delay it by a week. That particular day was their special time and I felt that it should be left to them.

A week later, the great day was upon us. My tummy wobbled and my knees shook. Notwithstanding all my thoughts about the corporate character of ministerial ordination, something in me wanted a private affair, just family and friends, but it was not to be.

I stumbled out of the vestry at the back of a long procession of choristers, hanging on to the elbow of the local parish priest (in the absence of my guide dog), and felt quite overcome by what I found. There were hundreds of people in the church!

I always imagined a few friends and family might come, but not this many. By the time the procession reached its destination, the worship had nearly lifted off the roof. The joy that rolled around the church was immeasurable. I was in tears before the procession, coming as it was from the back of the church, reached the front of the congregation.

I cried because I remembered the joy with which God had lifted me off my knees in that Christmas service years before. I cried because now I knew why. I cried with knowing I was standing with God on the end of a diving-board, about to leap into the unknown, a new life, a new operating partnership with him. And this was only being done, it could only be done, because God loved me and he was showing it.

The service was over in a flash, or so it seemed at the time, and soon afterwards we were back at The Well Centre, to entertain those who had come.

Funnily enough, my most abiding memory of that reception is of something which occurred afterwards. One of our sons had driven home quickly to fetch my guide dog. Rushing into The Well, Yates caught sight of me across the room. Suddenly this huge black Labrador crashed into my chest, and wrapped his front legs around my neck, his tail going round like a set of helicopter propeller blades. He said it all!

The next six months were marked by two noticeable changes at The Well. For some unknown reason, the word had spread remarkably rapidly. More and more people made the trip to South Wales. Was this the oil on the hinges?

It was not just that we were becoming busier receiving travellers from further afield; the atmosphere in The Well was changing. It was not only me and the team who were feeling it. Remarks about the atmosphere being somehow "different" became commonplace even among those visitors who did not profess Christianity. This change was to play on my mind for months, teasing me into an eventual recognition of its spiritual content.

The place was slowly and gently becoming "thin". This idea of a "thin" place can be traced right back to the earliest times of the Christian faith. The word describes a place which just seems somehow more transparent, a place where it seems easier to appreciate the presence of God. For fifteen years it has been the same. Those who walk in and immediately know that something is different, without being able to describe it, would find that word very appropriate.

Slowly, very slowly, I also was beginning to wonder, reflect and think the unthinkable about our models of healing ministry. I had met so many different types of people exercising healing ministry in all sorts of different ways, supposedly according to their individual calling, but it all seemed such hard work compared with the way it used to be in the New Testament.

Whatever version of the ministry I had learned or tried to turn my hand to, I was faced with frustration at the slowness, the apparent hesitation of God to help his people. I would spend as much of my time alone as I could, pondering the question of God's apparent reluctance and the possible reasons for it, but nothing came easily to mind.

I needed to get away and think.

CHAPTER 6
Echoes of Jesus

Changing my own mental model of Jesus and of his ministry took at least three pilgrimages to a little island called Bardsey before it started being straightened out in my mind.

Let me tell you a story about my changed perspective before sharing how the change came about. After my Bardsey revelations a Christian couple came to visit The Well, bringing with them their daughter Hannah who, by her own confession, was not a Christian.

Hannah's knees had both been smashed in a car accident some months earlier. She was still hobbling along slowly with the aid of two crutches but her wedding day was fast approaching. The three of them agreed that they could not even begin to imagine Hannah walking elegantly up the aisle on crutches on her wedding day!

The mother asked for prayer for Hannah. Hannah immediately felt it necessary to point out that she wasn't a Christian, assuming therefore that she was disqualified from receiving healing. Mistake number one! Here was the first wrong mental model of Jesus: that he would only do business with the already converted. There is no mention of conversion being a prerequisite to healing in the New Testament.

Dad then joined the conversation. "I don't know if you'll have any luck," he offered. "Hannah still has some forgiveness issues from her school days that she hasn't sorted out yet."

"Don't worry," I was then able to reply. "Jesus never suggested we would have to get our own spiritual lives sorted out first before he could heal us. That's just as well," I added, "or we'd all be in a pickle!"

Dad, cemented hard into his own mental model of a Jesus who would always demand spiritual improvement before giving gifts of grace, battled on. What about the man lowered down through the roof? "Jesus had to forgive him before he could heal him!" he announced triumphantly. He had missed the point of the story altogether and there was little time to start a lengthy discussion on it.

Suffice it to say, I managed to throw out a quick explanation. Matthew, Luke and Mark all tell the story of yet another miracle, the healing of the paralytic, which does not suggest we have to be forgiven before we can be healed, but simply demonstrates that Jesus' authority extends even to the forgiveness of sins. That is a different view of the story altogether. (See Matthew 9:1–8.)

The entire scene related in this Matthew passage is witnessed by the religious Jewish folk, the Pharisees and the scribes, who between them make an instant assessment of the situation. They agree that Jesus is making unique claims in that house that would have been blasphemous if they were untrue.

Later Judaic writings suggest God does not help liars or sinners. This poor man would definitely not, according to their theology, have walked away from his mat. Jesus would not have been able to heal him. The fact that he did meant that some type of magnificent and Godly power was manifestly operating through Jesus and that these other understandings of God were faulty.

So this miracle was not recorded to prove that we have to be forgiven of our sins before we can get healed but to remind us that Jesus does indeed have the Father's power flowing through him, both to forgive and to heal.

There was not the time for a profound discussion of the issues. I did not need Hannah to be filled up with any more doubt than she already had. "Just come with me," I offered to all three of them. "Come and sit in my office and we'll have a pray."

And so I began to worship God with thanksgiving. I thanked him for Jesus, for all he taught us and for all he had won for us on the cross. "Thank you, Father," I repeated, "that Jesus has taken all our pains and carried all our diseases and that by his wounds we are healed!"

By entering into worship and thanksgiving I was deliberately lifting Hannah's expectancy of the cross while at the same time defeating a few of Dad's doubts and all the while giving glory to the Father through Jesus.

In twenty minutes Hannah was up and jogging happily around our conference room. No crutches. It had been quite hard work but we had moved that little family sufficiently away from bad mental models of Jesus towards one in which they could receive what was already waiting for them in the kingdom of God. It's easy to write that now, that healing was already waiting for them, but I had only the vaguest idea of what that meant the day that Hannah's family came to call. That picture was to grow much clearer as we strode on down a new path of understanding. Much more would be revealed later.

But we were beginning to see the effect of bad mental modelling. Their mental model had within it an image of Jesus as being demanding and unpredictable, but the New Testament model displayed an image of him as being reliable and consistent.

I had by then spent years in ministry, working with the common mental model of an unreliable God, trying to discern what God was up to and trying to explain his reluctance to help. But all this would change.

This new perspective for me would come about as a result of my annual pilgrimage to Bardsey Island. It had become a joyfully anticipated event. The root of the name Bardsey, "The Island of Bards", has been traced back to the period of the Viking raids. This peaceful island – Ynys Enlli in the Welsh tongue, meaning "The Island in the Currents" – nestles in the swell of the Irish Sea, a few miles off the north-west tip of Wales.

When the Christians first arrived and took over the island in AD 546, St Cadfan and his companions built a monastery. It is now a ruin, but back then it was a mission beachhead.

The original pattern of the monks' life on the island would have been different from the traditions that guide the daily life of a contemporary monk or nun. There would have been a church at Bardsey's heart, but the monks themselves would have lived alone around the island in individual circular huts – which would have looked a bit like old-fashioned beehives.

Their religious life would have been very strict as well as physically and spiritually demanding. They would have been attending church services off and on throughout the night and during the day, and I can only guess that must have been pretty tough in the winter! Despite these hardships, people were attracted to the solitude and peace of the island, and many thousands have lived and died there down the years.

In the seventh century Ethelfrid's pagan army conquered Chester and destroyed the monastery at Bangor, not far away in North Wales. At least a thousand monks died in the carnage. Bardsey offered refuge to those who managed to flee from these outrages. Its remoteness and the treacherous waters that separate it from the mainland made it an ideal refuge.

Eventually, the form of monasticism with which we

are more familiar today was introduced to the island and the Augustinian Abbey of St Mary was built in the twelfth century. It is all in ruins now but the island remains a place of peaceful pilgrimage. I have found that it is much easier to take time to be aware of the presence of God when I am in such a remote place.

Over the centuries since the monks lived there in numbers, Bardsey in Wales became a kind of Iona in Scotland. That particular island is further north, on Scotland's western seaboard. It, too, has a wealth of ancient Christian history and tradition and is consequently a world-renowned place of pilgrimage.

About half a mile wide and three times as long, Bardsey has always been recognized as a healthy place.

Some clues as to the blessing and health associated with the island are found in the ancient history of that coast. Gerald de Barri was born of mixed Welsh and Norman blood and eventually became chaplain to King Henry II of England. He was a great twelfth-century cleric, traveller and writer. As Archdeacon of Brecon he toured Wales in 1188 with the Archbishop of Canterbury, Baldwin of Exeter, to raise support for the Third Crusade.

His writings about that journey, the *Itinerarium Cambriae* (1191) and the *Descriptio Cambriae* (1194), remain incredibly valuable historical documents, significant for their descriptions.

There he noted a discovery that no one on the island

of Bardsey died of anything other than old age. That would be quite an interesting claim even in the twenty-first century, but it was an earth-shattering claim during his long-ago lifetime!

In those days, people died of everything that was going: childbirth, children's illnesses, untreated wounds from the generally high level of social and military violence, and all manner of unknown and untreatable sickness that brought an early death to many.

In his writings, de Barri attributed the healthy life found on Bardsey to prayer. He believed this notable healing environment was entirely due to "the efficacious prayers of the saints".

As I travel there a keen anticipation marks the journey. In front of me are days and days of sea breezes and sunshine and early mornings, birdsong and afternoon naps, corporate worship in both the chapel and later in the farmhouse kitchen.

The heart of the visit, however, is the hours alone and the awareness of God's presence that one discovers. Taking time to think and to ponder and to wonder at the character and work of God is a transformational experience. I return annually, if I can, to rest and to sit on the rocky outcrops while the sea rolls in and washes the beach around my feet. I pause to let the gentle, salt-laden breeze bite deep into my skin, listen to the call of the pregnant and mother seals, and then talk with God.

Before I set foot on Bardsey for the first time, and

felt wrapped anew in the love of God that seems to come unfurling over the jetty as the boat makes landfall, I was actually a little wary of the prospect of the spartan existence that awaited me. I was about to "fall into God's arms" but was worried that my normal four-star hotel experience while travelling would ill equip me for such rigours. I teetered on the brink of not going.

I was struggling to imagine being on Bardsey Island without electricity. Bottled gas drove the cooker and fridge but candlelight and cold water sufficed for most other tasks. The whole thing sounded very risky for civilized man.

Even worse, I had heard – correctly, as it turned out – that there was no running water. A good trickle, which needed boiling and filtering, drifted down a pipe from a well on the mountainside to the cottages on the lower slopes – but that, together with a tank of rainwater, was it. So, no running water means no daily shower and no flush toilet. Horror upon horror! Can anyone survive like that?

I developed a mental picture of island life, a mental model of discomfort and hardship, which very nearly stopped me from going on pilgrimage that first time. By the end of my first week on Bardsey, that original and uncivilized mental model of island life had been almost entirely replaced by another one – a mental model of idyllic peace and closeness to the Almighty I had never even dreamed of.

Once there, the mental model of island life that I had

begun with stayed a while, trying to affect my behaviour. It had been formed out of two main sources: what I had been told and what I had already experienced.

I had been told to expect privation, not of food but certainly of facilities. I had been told that food and drink and a bed would be provided, but nothing else. I had been warned that too much time alone with oneself, if a person is not accustomed to it, can eventually create enormous anxieties which make one most uncomfortable, if not distressed.

To this list of bad news I quickly added my young memories of camping: being vulnerable to the elements; attending to one's personal toiletry in the woods; and eating mass-produced food and green custard that gave us all stomach cramps – all of it stinking of campfire smoke!

If I had stuck with that original model, developed from what I had been told and experienced for myself, I might never have gone to Bardsey. Now that I know the second mental model, built out of my actual experience of island pilgrimage, I have difficulty staying away. Interestingly, our mental models, the way in which we perceive truth, can be dramatically changed by our experiences, and our behaviour is governed accordingly.

Unhappily, many questions about the healing aspects of kingdom life, and the King at its heart, do not see the light of day. They don't turn into meaningful answers, let alone strategic actions by the church, because these ideas are often too different from the mental models of

Jesus which might be prevailing in a particular branch of God's family.

I have since recognized that old and well-established mental models of Jesus can be very powerful in acting as a brake on our ability to consider new insights, let alone to take them on board. They are deeply ingrained images that leaders of any church organization tend to hold on to quite subconsciously, often failing to refocus, even when presented with clear scriptural evidence to the contrary.

They can be shaped by our upbringing, our churchmanship, and by our experience as praying Christians. The trouble with experience is that it gets in the way and attacks childlike trust.

The general mental model of Christ I had found in the church was of someone who was a little reluctant, if not generally unenthusiastic, about helping his followers out of trouble. This did not compare, in my view, with the New Testament account of Christ who, in his compassion, readily offered healing to all who asked him.

And how can we honestly say that we trust Jesus when we have absolutely no idea of what he will do in answer to prayer? This is a terribly important question for any would-be miracle worker to answer, as insufficient trust means few miracles, and the scarcity of miracles we see in the church today is probably the result of insufficient trust.

One student of Jesus' ministry reported to me around that time: "Once I was asked to pray for five little boys, all aged about six years old, who had cancer of the blood. Four died soon afterwards and the fifth went into remission for a year and then went on to glory."

To a greater or a lesser extent, this is a heartbreaking experience commonly encountered by many a praying Christian.

"I received five large blows to my trust that God would restore life, as each one died," he continued. He was still trying to come to terms with God's mysterious and apparent failure to save these children.

Much second-guessing about God's intentions in this sort of thing has been drip fed to many of us over the years by friends and family. The end result is always the same: our image of Jesus, our mental model of him, is tarnished. We cannot help this – we are, after all, human beings.

We begin to know from our experience that persuading God to restore anything is not easy, and we start to think our compassionate God rarely responds in the way we think he should. We build our own personal theologies accordingly.

"But now I know in my heart," said my Christian friend, "that the real Christ, the Jesus revealed in the pages of the Gospels rather than the image of him that I had built out of my own experiences, never failed to bring quick and complete restoration to all who came and asked him – with as little as a mustard seed of expectancy that he would do it."

How had a change in my own thinking come about?

On one of those atmospheric mornings on the island, I began to stumble across one of the major keys to the world of miraculous Christianity. It was going to be something very exciting and very new to me.

Of course, I had by then crossed paths with hundreds of faithful Christians who confessed a miraculous faith experience, but on closer examination so much of what they had witnessed simply did not seem to be fulfilling the New Testament promise of a dynamic kingdom that changed lives in droves whenever it came near. Things happen here and there, in ones and twos, but rarely in New Testament proportions.

Many of the episodes being related were from other people's experiences rather than their own. The uncomfortable truth I had taken to Bardsey that first year, deep in the secret recesses of my mind, was that we ordinary people in the church are simply not experiencing miracles in New Testament proportions, and that has probably been the case for many centuries.

The New Testament reveals how Christians are to be involved in healing the sick in Jesus' name, but our practice seems to have slowed right down and become most hesitant and reluctant. Our healing – and our evangelism – seemed to me to be very short of breath!

There was an enormous amount of hard work going on in and around church life in these areas. If the truth be told, that was my problem: I was having difficulty with the words "hard work". My reading of the New Testament was suggesting to me that in those days these activities were a lot less complicated and far more common.

There have been numerous times in recent history when God's foot appeared to be tweaking the accelerator but the car seemed, on the whole, to be stuck in first gear.

God often gives me hints and nudges about things to explore and investigate. One particular morning on Bardsey, a big one was on the way. I was leaning on my elbows on the old drystone wall outside the front door of one of the island's old farmhouses, hot coffee mug in hand, when it arrived. My feet were planted firmly on a gravel path which ran across the front of the house and away to my right, towards the old farm buildings that had served for many years as a hermitage. To my left the path led to the cottage garden gate, through to the garden with its high, flowering hedges and its well-trodden path, across the lawn to the *ty-bach*, the "little house" at the bottom of the garden.

The sea breeze had calmed itself as the sun came up, and the fresh morning air was filled with the comforting sound of buzzing bees, punctuated by the intermittent bleating of sheep. Beyond the chest-high cottage wall on which I was leaning, topped with flat stones that were warming up nicely in the sunshine, the ground sloped gently upwards across the field away from me. Through the old gate, and beyond the rough, rutted tractor track that serves as the island's main road, it rose sharply to form the gorse and bracken covered mountain that forms most of the eastern shoreline and reaches up to scrape the scurrying clouds above its shoulders.

Slightly over to the right, as I raised my eyes and ears in the direction of the mountain, the sun warmed my face and gladdened my heart. I relaxed, deeply aware that God was in heaven, and that all was well.

This peaceful Bardsey morning, as on every morning in summer, there was birdsong. The sound of a combustion engine on the island is limited to the farmer's daily tractor trip up the lane and no telephone ever rings within earshot. No car ever comes speeding past, shaking and vibrating to deafening bass notes from the speakers of its sound system. This is the quiet and peaceful rural life, much as it would have been 150 years ago.

Among the sounds which would have been unfamiliar to urban ears on this particular day, two skylarks were talking to each other across the field in front of me. At least I supposed that was what they were up to, and I was privileged to be sandwiched between them, listening in on their conversation.

I leaned forward, forearms resting on the flat stones that levelled the top of the wall, sipping my coffee and listening to them. It took ten minutes or so for me to realize it, but I slowly became aware that one was calling and the other was repeating his call. The originator was somewhere ahead of me, up across the rugged path, in the bracken and bushes of the lower slopes of the mountain.

The bird copying was very close, sitting in the hedge along the *ty-bach* path that ran away through the garden gate to my left.

Each bird's stock of notes amounted to only five or six individually distinct sounds, which were being sung in varied order, with varying gaps in between. Like ringing the changes of church bells, the combinations seemed endless.

After every slightly differing call instigated by my new-found friend ahead of me at the foot of the mountain, there followed a pause for what I guessed was the collecting of bird thoughts. Then the skylark in the hedge along the path to my left would repeat the call, note for note, exactly as it had been sung a quarter of a mile away to my front. Then the call would change again, and then again be faultlessly repeated.

I remained still, hearing every note in the peaceful air and marvelling at the exchange. Twenty minutes passed and still they were calling to each other – the same mountainside bird originating each different call and the same garden bird repeating it, note for note, in the clear and still air. Eventually – slowly at first, as I was so engrossed in the birds' musical conversation – I thought I was beginning to see what God could be saying to me.

It seemed that his intention was that we should become something like an echo. As the bird which was beside me echoed exactly the bird in front of me, across the rising slope of the hayfield, so we should attempt to be echoes of Christ's message and ministry. Might the miraculous life be restored in the church if we all set out to copy Christ's healing ministry?

At first I shrugged off the thought of being a "Jesus echo". It sounded almost as if it was going to be the same tired, old and simplistic Sunday school message we had been sharing with mainland church people for as long as the island had been in Christian use. How often had I heard someone pronounce that we should all be striving to be more Jesus-like? Set in that context, what I was hearing began to seem an insignificant idea. Many more learned people had announced our need for Christ-likeness more often, to more people in more pews and from higher pulpits than I could.

But then the more I listened, the more sense it made. In fact, this message had a simple substance to it that felt very different and needed understanding at a deeper level altogether. This was not the same old and rather vaguely encouraging message that we should be Christlike in the community by being nice to people (valuable though that is).

This was a different and deeper thought entirely. This was a calling to copy. Not a calling to copy what the modern church was teaching us about healing ministry, with all its variety and different possibilities, but to copy Jesus himself in his ministry.

But wasn't I doing that anyway? Surely I had been taught properly over the years and had built up quite a body of experience. I could see only one thing wrong with the way we were doing healing ministry: it didn't work very well! We may have varied theological understandings and techniques but, compared to the disciples' experiences recorded in the New Testament, we were really not seeing enough miracles.

We often recognize this reality but if we are not in complete denial about it, we often take it as a spur to continue the search for yet more complexities in our healing theology.

I began to wonder: was the church now teaching itself by listening to itself and not to the Scriptures? Was it developing by drawing in thought patterns from secular skills and practices rather than through a deeper reverence for the truth of the original New Testament ways?

Here lies the danger of pilgrimage! It can open one up to all sorts of ideas one would not have dreamed of in the hustle and bustle of daily life back home.

But the skylarks went on calling, and the message to me that morning was insistent, unsteadying, if not troubling: "Go back! Start again and be an echo of Christ's ministry. Imitate his ministry!" Well, that would be quite an adventure!

It felt like a call to disrobe, to fling off so much which books and helpful friends had taught; to strip away the outer garments that innumerable lecturers and healing theologians had taught and to start all over again.

I was gaining a real sense that I would have to discard

the old and comparatively ineffective clothes of modern healing ministry, and return to Christ's teaching alone before we could see miraculous Christianity at work again in New Testament proportions.

The thought of such an adventure was most unsettling. I had been working full time in the healing ministry, involved in practices taught me by the well known and the most experienced. My ministry was unthreatening and quite acceptable.

No one, to use the vernacular, was giving me any "aggro". To get better I could simply learn more secular counselling skills, Christianize them with prayer and a few proof texts, and then absorb them into my way of doing things. Was there a problem with this approach?

My inbuilt and quite natural defence mechanisms clicked in immediately, reassuring me that all I was doing in ministry was already Christ-centred. Why was there a need to change?

There was initially just that one reason that I kept thinking about again: by and large, healing ministry today does not work very well. Although I would tell of the magnificent true accounts of lives made whole, the awful truth was that I never told the stories about those who weren't healed. Quite honestly, I knew a great deal more of the latter than the former. I also knew that I shared that knowledge with many other Christians who minister for healing.

It can be hard to admit to such "failures", as to do

so is sometimes taken as being critical and judgmental towards the church. Many consider such disloyal thinking to be a cardinal sin, if not downright heretical! So we don't go there. But here on pilgrimage I was definitely, albeit tentatively, sticking a toe in the water of divergent thinking.

Leaving the buzzing bees in the garden and my empty coffee mug in the kitchen, I climbed the stairs and sat down on the side of my bed, kicking off my shoes and searching for comprehension. I felt on the verge of something that would look to most like a shallow and insignificant pavement edge, but it was feeling like a cliff top. How could I discover the width of the leap ahead?

Did I have the childlike courage to explore? Could I be deaf to my slowly but steadily acquired experience and kingdom knowledge and be prepared to start again? Not to put too fine a point on it, was I ready to jeopardize or even sacrifice the ministry reputation I had gained so far?

CHAPTER 7
Fields White Unto Harvest

We had mobilized a prayer army for our friend Shirley, but all our efforts were to no avail. Her funeral was the breaking point, a pivotal moment for the whole of my ministry.

One of our founding team members reported to us one day that his wife, Shirley, had lung cancer. The news about her was bad and all who knew her were devastated. But, being married to a founder member of our young ministry team, she was always going to be surrounded by those willing to pray for her healing.

It took a little over a year for her to die. While her husband and her son came to terms with what was unfolding, hundreds of us, willingly, hopefully and lovingly, applied our shoulders to the wheel in prayer. We were determined that this disease would not happen. Prayer chains were formed; vigils were volunteered; sacraments became a regular part of her daily life. Bishops anointed her with oil, and candles were lit in far-flung churches. Intercessors heard from heaven that she would live but prophets heard, apparently from the same source, that she would not.

As the months rolled on, her close friends lovingly and prayerfully tried everything we knew about the healing ministry. We trawled back through all the hours and hours of teaching we had received to find the clue. We went to new lectures on root causes and pored over and over the tapes of old ones, praying and hoping for just one give-away sentence, one spark in the darkness that might reveal whatever might be the block that was preventing Shirley's healing.

When we could not find the key to turn in her particular lock, we fell into that deep trough of dark and commonly believed error that supposes there must be some unconfessed sin lurking from the past that God cannot work around. Failing that, we were even tempted at one point to reach for the blunt instrument of deliverance ministry, often the weapon of last resort for those who feel a sense of ministerial responsibility but are lost in a sense of inadequacy.

"O Jesus, answer us!" we pleaded. But there was no response; no one answered. We retreated into sacramental ministries and pseudo-prophetic guesswork of every kind.

There was not a technique we missed. What were we doing wrong? We wondered: Why could we not get God to get rid of this thing? Should we be shouting louder? Should we be making bigger prayer chains? Should we have them all praying in waves? Surely he is Almighty God! Perhaps he is deep in thought or busy? Perhaps he is sleeping, like Jesus in the storm-shaken boat, and has to be woken up somehow?

All we could do was pray more firmly, more strongly, more fiercely, more emotionally, but nothing we could see was stirring in heaven. Almighty God – our own God of grace and power and healing – appeared to have deserted her. Did he have a plan? Perhaps he had a secret script for all this, in which her dying played a vital and irreplaceable role? Could he not tell us what it was? What, I wondered, was the point of saving the world if he was only going to devise plans for us that were beyond our understanding and deepened our pain?

At Shirley's funeral, in the middle of all the bursting pain of emptiness and agonizing loss, amid so much celebration of her life, I climbed down from my Christian pride box and my assumption that I knew all there is to know about healing theology.

I got angry. What had happened to the kingdom of God? Jesus was continually talking about "the kingdom of heaven". The gospel was originally known as the gospel of the kingdom and the first disciples went everywhere preaching it. It is the only subject on which Jesus taught systematically. Yet these kingdom dynamics are an almost forgotten subject: not taught, not understood, and seldom mentioned.

The contemporary European church has neglected

her task and calling to teach and preach the restoring kingdom and the powerful healing message of the cross. Instead we have been busy for centuries justifying ourselves in reducing our own original high purposes to the somewhat lower levels of civilizing the world, acquiring wealth, developing imposing rituals, erecting and maintaining magnificent buildings and invoking God's blessing on opposing armies in times of war.

Looking around me at the sadness and the bewilderment in that church, it felt like there was an atmosphere of antiquity. The careful rituals conveyed a great dignity but there was a danger that they might seem completely irrelevant. Religion is failing when it cannot speak to people where they are in real life. A ministry of healing is worthless unless it affects men and women where they actually hurt. If I have arthritis and Jesus heals today, then I need to know how to invite the kingdom into my arthritic body.

The congregation around me were singing songs of praise and saying prayers of thankfulness and I was asking myself, "Why is healing so difficult for such a loving, powerful God?" But for me this was not a time to try to work it out. This was a time for recognizing reality, abasement and anguished confession.

"Where now is the Lord, the God of Elijah?" I yelled under my breath during that funeral service. Elijah had seen the fire of God come down with comparative ease and burn up his offering on Mount Carmel; where was God now?

Elisha's heartfelt cry was an easy one to echo. Standing there in the middle of Shirley's funeral service, something about the Christian healing ministry dawned on me, not gently growing like some hard-sought revelation but with the brightness and crash of lightning. It was a shocking contrast to my own ministry (and the ministry of the church as a whole, with only a few dazzling exceptions).

Jesus had found it relatively easy to heal the sick in his day. Had this been because he was also God? Well, the apostles found it comparatively easy as well and so did the elders and the early deacons and, it would seem, almost every Christian in the early church, too!

In those far-off days it would have been possible to recognize a Christian by the apparent ease with which the sick around them were healed. People could tell an apostle by the signs and wonders that he did! The disciples of Jesus were known to lay their hands on the sick – who then became well again.

But by the end of the service I was racked with the feeling that this was no longer true for me – nor for most other Christians I knew, either. The Spirit of Christ worked at will in the early church. Since then there had been some miracles, but where is the love and the fairness in singling out only a few?

Has God ceased to heal? What has happened to make him so reluctant to help his followers? Had all that teaching I had received over the years been wasted? Had I missed some important issue here? Was there something badly wrong in me, or in our beloved sister Shirley, that God found it impossible to work through?

Had I not inherited, because of Calvary, a robe of righteousness to cover my filthiness? This being the case, why can God not work through me? If not through me, was there not a tiny window of holiness in all the hundreds of people and the weight of their prayers, booming upwards through their tears in the long months of Shirley's illness, that could have provoked him to heal?

Such was the boiling feeling in my raging heart during Shirley's funeral service. Nothing of this could be spoken out; times like these are too full of other people's pain and deep need of God.

It seemed best that this angry soul, on the end of a packed church pew, should keep his own counsel. But those outraged feelings, in content though not in depth, never left me.

"Dear God," I begged over my sandwiches one busy conference lunchtime later that summer, "the way we do it in the church just doesn't seem to work very well at all. I have learned so much over my years of working for you and yet I seem to know nothing. When the chips are down, there is absolutely nothing the church can do about it but deliver a lot of platitudes, and sound very spiritual in the process.

"I have seen your glorious hand in healing many a spiritual or emotional problem, but the need for you to get involved again in physical illness is nothing short of staggering! The ministry of healing has become a ministry of praying *for* people, if the truth be known, but Jesus didn't pray for the sick, he actually healed them! The world is brimming over with sickness of every kind imaginable; we are crying out for you to be like you used to be. You used to do it but now it is all so rare! Now all we can do is wonder: Why not?

"Now we spend all our time trying to work out theological and philosophical sounding excuses for failure. Of course we cannot call it your failure because you are omnipotent and omniscient and therefore you cannot fail. But it seems as though you failed Shirley and thousands like her – and the hundreds of us who begged you to move.

"The church has also taught us that you never change, yet you surely seem to. There was a day when you healed everyone who asked Jesus and now you do not. They tell us that you are unconditional love, and yet you heal one or two and not the majority. Is that love? You say that your yoke is light, but you seem to let us down all the time. The one simple, sought-after gift that Jesus gave away so readily now causes more pain and doubt and argument about you than anything else I know. So show me your glory! The question I have for you is this: As the church does not know how to do it like you did it, how did you do it, and how did you teach it so effectively? What did you teach about healing? What, for the sake of the glory of Christ, have we lost?"

For half an hour I ranted and raved like this and beat on the gates of heaven. By the end of that lunch break my healing ministry, as I knew it, had died. Deep down in the bottom of things, too deep to admit it fully even to myself, it died. No one even suspected it except me and God and a few chosen friends, but everything I had learned from the church over ten years of full-time healing ministry slipped silently into the grave.

I gave it up because it didn't work. I threw away a model of ministry that had become so complicated that no one could understand it any more. The people didn't understand what was going on and the church leaders didn't understand much of it, either. What seems to have started out as a "Yes, come here!" sort of ministry has been turned by the church into a mystery. Now we no longer know how it works or why it doesn't. It builds up hopes and dashes them with disappointment.

But in the same way that a new seed lies on the ground, encased in the rotting remains of a once glorious fruit, it was then, amazingly and beyond comprehension, that the light of Christ began to flood the darkness.

The results of that small but possibly outrageous prayer turned out to be something so huge and so different that it shakes those who pray for the sick with disease-shattering simple truth. My ministry and my life were about to turn upside down. We were about to be launched on a whole new voyage, a new journey across uncharted seas with many battles to fight and many more victories to win.

We started out on the voyage that afternoon. The seed of those outrageous prayers had already begun to germinate. In a second teaching session that very afternoon, after the sandwiches and my prayer of ministry surrender, we were pleasantly surprised to find every seat taken for the afternoon session. The room had been peppered with empty seats at the morning session but expectant folk kept coming in with smiling, happily chatting faces and soon filled the aisles and the space across the back of the platform behind me.

The place was humming with anticipation. It was packed and I didn't know why. It was great to see them all but I could not help thinking, "What's going on, here?" It sounded to me as if I was standing in the middle of a summer swarm of bees. The optimistic conversation seemed unstoppable.

The guitar player had not, as promised, turned up to lead us in singing, so we said one psalm together as a gathering act of worship and then, with nothing to lose and with all my courage ebbing away and out through the toes of my boots, I took a deep breath and asked the audience a simple question:

"Jesus gave gifts of healing to everyone who asked him, and God is love, and God doesn't change. So who needs a miracle in their life this afternoon?"

There came a surprised pause. I was expecting doubtful hesitation more than anything else. I was expecting the three ubiquitous ladies with sick relatives in New Zealand or some other far-flung land that often populate healing meetings to step forward, but the room seemed suddenly filled with waving hands, like wind-blown barley stalks in a field white for harvest.

At first I still felt the boldness of the challenge I had thrown out to them, but soon became very scared. I wanted to panic. I checked with myself that I knew exactly where the door was in case I needed to make a fast exit. If God did not turn up at this point, my ministry would be well and truly ruined! Well, that would not be much of a loss, I managed to smile to myself – it doesn't work very well anyway! Hadn't I just been trying to give it back to God?

Well, in for a penny, in for a pound, I thought. I began to preach the good news of the nature and character of the kingdom by reminding them that Jesus Christ healed everyone who asked him – everyone, that is, with a modicum of expectant faith, and he repeatedly told us that he could only do what the Father was doing:

> *Don't you believe that I am in the Father, and*
> *that the Father is in me? The words I say to you*
> *are not just my own. Rather, it is the Father, living*
> *in me, who is doing his work.*

JOHN 14:10

Then again, the only people I could find in the New Testament who did not receive healing were those who did not ask Jesus for it.

I drew the simple conclusion from these facts that God's will must be to heal all who come to Jesus for restoration. "That might not be your experience," I told them, "but it's the biblical truth! So either the Bible is wrong or your experiences are not valid. Take your pick!"

And then it was God himself who took the opportunity to demonstrate his grace at that point. I had no more to say to them and little to do with what followed. There was an agonizing silence for what seemed like forever, but in reality the audience's surprise only lasted a few seconds. It was almost as if they had never been spoken to like that before. They probably hadn't.

Then, to coin a phrase, all heaven was let loose. Skin complaints began to clear up, chronic stomach and chest pain disappeared, a fused spine became flexible, pain free and pliable. One lady stood without sticks for the first time in twenty years. Another lady with a muscle-wasting disease stopped shaking. One case of toothache died away and one man's damaged knee ligaments were completely restored so that he was able to return to work the following Monday morning after spending three months on sick leave.

One person walking past the conference room outside the building received healing for a bad back, without any prayer at all, and two ladies were freed from the pain of arthritic knees quite spontaneously while sitting next to each other watching it all from the back of the room.

That was the first time we saw what we came to know as "shadow healing", a feature of the kingdom which bears a further mention. Fearful? Frightening? To be avoided at all cost? Did the people in that room think so? They were being healed. If we truly have the Spirit of Christ within, how can we do anything but rejoice with them?

Why should this sort of thing be happening? It would take months and years of study, of meditational prayer, of discussion and experience before we were to see the fullness of what God has to offer the world and why these miracles of healing would break out in this way.

We were to slowly rediscover a spiritual truth which we had never been taught on too many courses to mention, and it's this. Our simple prayers and complicated ministry techniques are of little kingdom value. Isaiah describes them (as well as much else, of course) in his chapter 64 (verse 6). He writes:

> *All of us have become like one who is unclean, and all our righteous acts are like filthy rags; we all shrivel up like a leaf, and like the wind our sins sweep us away.*

And yet working with him instead of for him, working in tandem with him, we can be effective kingdom workers; we can reflect something of Jesus. We began that day to rediscover the tandem working arrangement that God had planned for his disciples all along: that our job is to preach the kingdom and the cross in its fullness, and he would then support the truth we speak with corresponding signs that we would all wonder at. We are to rightly preach the message of the cross, and its power will heal the sick. And it does!

> *For the message of the cross is foolishness to those who are perishing, but to us who are being saved it is the power of God.*
>
> 1 CORINTHIANS 1:18

> *And having disarmed the powers and authorities, he made a public spectacle of them, triumphing over them by the cross.*
>
> COLOSSIANS 2:15

Standing on the lecture platform that afternoon, I saw all this in quantities that are rarely seen, amid a joy rarely experienced. For the very first time we had begun to see a New Testament ministry in New Testament proportions. The river of grace was in spate!

The journey home from that conference should normally take about an hour and a half by road. It felt as though it took five minutes. What had happened? Why, after all these years of hard, dead-horse-flogging, theorizing, excuse-making, sacrificial, heart-breaking praying for the sick, had it suddenly become comparatively easy? What had we done? If God does not change, then we must have done. But how?

On the trip home that evening we made long lists in the car of everyone we had prayed for and noted who had seen a noticeable improvement before the afternoon was out. Somewhere in excess of a third of all those waving hands had recognized improvement in their various conditions. It was a start. Added to those, of course, would be the illnesses that cannot be measured on the spot without medical examination, and those that were to take a while longer to mend.

We were elated. As far as we were aware, this type of healing in such significant numbers was not the norm in the vast majority of churches – and yet here it was, right in front of us. The whole event had been a miracle made out of miracles. We must, we joyfully proclaimed the whole way home, find out more and teach more so that everyone can share in it!

Since then there have been thousands of healing services and countless teaching schools and conferences around the world, and the healing power of God goes on working. The number of the sick and the injured able to receive relief and restoration has increased considerably since then. Everywhere the good news of the kingdom is fully preached, the miracles confirm it.

And as for Shirley's husband? I asked him, not long after he had watched and ministered at that first fruitful conference talk, if he was angry that all this had not happened eighteen months earlier.

He must be thinking, I suggested to him, that had we fallen into this miraculous life of miracle working a year earlier than we did, there might have been a chance that Shirley might still be alive. But, so full of wisdom as he always is, he gently explained to me that he sees God's desire to heal as rather like penicillin.

It has existed since the beginning of time but we have only recently discovered it. There is no future in remorse for the millions who could have been saved by it before its discovery – we simply rejoice that we have found it at last!

Ten years and thousands of healing miracles later, we know what happened that day. We were prepared to throw away all our concepts about a healing God and take a giant step of trust into the relatively unknown.

As for the "shadow" healing that we first saw that day, this must surely be one of the greatest delights we have yet found in this kingdom ministry. This particular type of miracle has gained its name from Acts 5:15. People were bringing the sick into the streets on beds and mats and laying them on the pavements, "so that at least Peter's shadow might fall on some of them as he passed by." They were all healed. There was no prayer recorded here and Jesus had ascended to heaven a while earlier. Yet they were all healed.

We find that during the preaching of the good news of the kingdom many are healed quite spontaneously without any prayer being said for them. It is not unusual to see damaged neck vertebrae restored, bent and battered fingers straightened, arthritic hands renewed, asthma disappearing, withered hands rebuilt, hearing given and skin complaints vanishing away without any recourse to ministry. No one prays. The hearers are simply washed with the truth about Jesus' cross and his kingdom, the living word of God.

Why should this "shadow" healing be one of the greatest delights of healing ministry today? Because when spontaneous healing breaks out there cannot be any doubt at all in anyone's mind as to who is doing the work. And God himself is making sure that no one doubts it!

My heart was gladdened by this new wave of Spirit activity in our ministry, but my confusion was still not totally resolved. Shirley's dying had confused me; the myriad of ministry styles in the church had confused me; the biblical truth that God doesn't change, compared with his obvious reluctance to heal today, had confused me.

We had fallen into something very different. What was it? I began to find my answers down in Devon, at the side of that estuary where I had spent so many happy days, so many years before.

CHAPTER 8

Crossing My Own Personal Jordan

I suppose that confusion over this kingdom business is hardly surprising. Jesus teaches us that we will only be able to see the kingdom if we approach it in a childlike manner. There has to be a simplicity of spirit.

That is where my estuary vision came in useful, twelve years before writing this. It helped me to see the difference between the historical ministry of the church in the area of healing and the wonderful gift of simple kingdom living and its consequences.

I remember the vision as if it were given yesterday. Its backdrop was the memory of the quiet estuary of my Devon youth, with its wooded hillsides, its quaint shoreline stone cottages and the slapping halyards of the sailing boats in the evening river breezes.

If I lean back and shut my eyes, the picture returns. But now I am standing knee-deep in its cool waters, some three feet from the bank, roasting in the afternoon heat on my back and the reflecting rays of the sun coming off the surface of the water onto my arms and face. I am fighting a sense of sinking in my heart as I allow my gaze to drift up and down the riverbank in front of me; all away to my left and down to my right there are plants wilting and dying in the direct glare of the sun, the parched heat and the dry soil.

So near and yet so far – rows and rows of plants only a few inches from the water's edge and yet drying out and dying out in the heat of the day. And so it is to have compassion for the sick and injured among us. I must minister to them in the only way I know how. I bend down, scooping my cupped hands up from between my knees and splashing the nearest plants with the healing, cooling water they need in order to survive. I seem to do this a hundred, if not a thousand times, while my back seems as if it is breaking and I am simply not satisfied with the results.

When my salty, stinging tears of exasperation eventually begin to flow down from my sore eyes and mix themselves with the handfuls of water, the nearest plants develop darker brown earth around them and in time, some of them seem to recover slightly.

I stand up to stretch my muscles, my back aching from the work, and wipe my sleeve across my streaming forehead. I glance up and down the bank again at the acres of suffering plants, and return stiffly to my labours.

Retrieving my watch from my pocket, I look at it quickly. Another two hours or so and I can go home, secure in the knowledge that I will have done my best for another day. I swallow down the thought that I will most likely have failed many more plants than I will be able to rescue, but then, how can I be expected to do everything around here? After all, I am only one among many. I cannot see, from my spot in the river, any colleagues in ministry, but I am sure they must be around somewhere.

As far as I can see, I am doing the job aright. I am metaphorically standing in the river of God's saving grace and doing my little bit to pastor, through that grace, the ones nearest to me. This is all a man can do. Anyway, I am taught to be humble – I must not assume in any way that the success of the kingdom or its ministry depends on me.

In a little while I straighten up again, stretching my shoulders backwards and arching my spine to ease the muscle stiffness in them. But who comes here? From away to my right through the heat haze emerges a rider, his shimmering white horse walking along the riverside path towards me. I use his coming to wait and rest, pausing on the off chance that conversation might take place.

Hoof beat by hoof beat, he slowly approaches, and then, as he reaches me, he reins in his horse and leans slowly forward, face turned towards me and forearms resting on the pommel. The broad brim of his hat obscures much of his face in shadow.

"Good afternoon, sir," I offer.

"May I ask what you are doing?" he enquires of me.

"I was walking along here this morning," I tell him, "and caught sight of all these lovely plants and flowers up and down the riverbank. They were doing very badly in the heat of the day. They were suffering and dying, and yet all they were doing was just being here! I wanted to help, so I climbed into the river and began to scoop water. I have no bucket or hose, only my hands. I suppose that's all right because it's the water that does the refreshing, not me! But now my back is getting the better of me, so I shall stop soon and go home for a rest."

Without taking his eyes off me for a moment, he raises himself upright again in the saddle and says, "Follow me!"

"Who are you?" I ask him in turn. I am tired and hot and dirty and I want to go home. If I'm going to follow someone at this point on such a dusty and exhausting day, heaven only knows where, I would need to know what I am going to let myself in for. So I hesitate.

The rider waves a hand along the far estuary bank, all the way along in one direction and back along the near bank. "All this is mine." He is smiling fondly at the whole vista of browns and greens and blues in front of him when he says this.

"The river is mine and the ground to either side is mine. Where the estuary comes from is mine and where it flows into the sea is mine. The air above it is mine and the plants are mine. Follow me and I will show you something."

So I do. It seems uncomfortable to be carried along like this; I was right to do what I had been doing, I was right to be where I was, and now it is right to go home. But I take a step of faith. This is against my better judgment, but I take the step, nevertheless. His words seem to want to direct my path.

I climb and slip unsteadily back up the bank and roll down my trouser legs. I slip my socks and shoes on again as he applies his heels and the white horse sets off at a steady walking pace, the rider never looking back to see if I am following. And so we go on for a little while, no one speaking. I am finding strength and support in the sweltering heat by pacing my footsteps in the rhythm of the horse's hooves. Straight on we go for over a mile, turning to the right as we follow the line of the river around a wide bend to a place where it widens out even further, between the wooded hillsides that have a boat-house nestled at their feet.

"There," he points out to me, "in that boat-house is a gift for you. You have worked hard on my river and you have worked well with my flowers, but now I have a reward for you. Enjoy it and you will learn something."

Intrigued, I climb down the wooded slope until I reach the boat-house door, left unlocked, slightly ajar and welcoming. Inside is a sight that takes my breath away. Lying there quietly, waiting for me, is the sleekest and most beautiful speed-boat I have ever seen. It has two mighty motors mounted on its stern, and the painter is cast loose in readiness for me. I turn to wave my thanks to the rider, but of course he is gone.

The main boat-house doors are lying open onto the water. Both engines roar and leap into life at my touch. The bow lifts to the wooded banks on the other side, and the stern sinks as the propeller blades bite deep.

Managing to stay upright under the forces of acceleration, I throw the tiller to one side and we are away upriver, white water boiling behind me, wind playing with my hair and keeping my face cool as the sharp evening sun burns down.

I roar very quickly upriver until it seems right to turn the boat around. The engines soften and the bow turns, only to rise again towards the sky as I let the engines have their freedom. Soon I am racing past the boat-house again on our way downstream and all thoughts of strain and stress are gone. Anxiety has left me and my aching shoulders are beginning to recover their strength after the day's toil.

All is well. I open the throttles as far as they will go – this is the stuff that any boy's adventure is made of! As the way ahead appears empty, safe and clear for a moment, I turn around to look behind, and thrill with the sight that meets my eyes. The blue-white waves, one issuing from either side of the stern, broaden and widen out behind me as I go, until, a long way behind me they reach the bank. This wall of water is quite high enough to fling itself far up the dry earth bank and the deluge completely swamps every plant, every struggling and suffering flower and weed alike, almost up as high as the rider's footpath, and certainly for the entire length of the river. To complete my joy for them all, the other wave soaks and nearly drowns the opposite bank to exactly the same extent.

And how much effort have I put in now to saving the plants? None at all. All I have done is enjoy myself in taking the fullest advantage of the gift of the boat and access to the river.

So then it begins to dawn on me – effective ministry will never be a function of how hard I work or how cleverly I work. It will be the fruit of my living in the kingdom and enjoying it to the full. The realization of this truth is stunning. I have never even heard a whisper of it before.

I cut the engines and we glide gently to a halt in the quiet of the river. There is no sign of the rider anywhere along either bank, but I can only fall to my knees in the bottom of the boat and thank him for this revelation. I would never have imagined that I could have watered the banks in that dramatically effective way.

In the space of a few moments he had allowed me a glimpse of the power of the message of the cross: it had begun to dawn on me that a heaven- and earth-shaking exchange had taken place on that "green hill far away", that our difficulties, troubles, pain and sickness in this world could all be freely exchanged there for what I later recognized as a whole list of Gifts of Calvary (see the "Gifts of Calvary" appendix).

And my role in all this? He taught me in that picture that all I need to do is to thank him and praise him, and enjoy my kingdom living in the shadow of the cross – and the plants around me will in their turn receive in my wake.

"But all this is too easy!" I shout towards the wooded riverbank in the hope that he might hear me, but there is no answer. His silence seems like the deep and contented acceptance of heaven.

The lesson of the estuary vision is clear – the regular and consistent healing of the sick is not best achieved through one particular ministry method or another, nor by choice of ritual, nor by deeds and actions, nor even necessarily by petition prayer. It will not have escaped the reader's attention that consistent results by any of these modern or traditional means are nothing short of grinding hard work, if indeed such a successful ministry is possible at all.

I had been shown something that I badly needed to know before any healing ministry could really work through me to any sizeable and reliable degree. I had just been shown that divine healing is not a ministry after all, it is the natural outworking of being an everyday disciple.

It is the natural kingdom dynamic that results from the bold and full preaching of the good news of kingdom and cross. If anything, we should be starting to think of healing as not being a subject in its own right but as part of the ministry of the word. Messing about in the river up to my knees was a picture of a minister trying his best to disseminate grace. Driving up and down in the speed-boat is a picture of a disciple enjoying his true kingdom role, that of proclamation of kingdom and cross.

And, as a result, I was now looking forward to enjoying praising and giving thanks for all that Jesus has done and showed us, living in the kingdom to the utmost and rejoicing as people receive healing in a disciple's wake.

Had I begun to find one of the lost secrets of the kingdom? How intriguing! I knew there were such things:

> *He [Jesus] said, "The knowledge of the secrets of the kingdom of God has been given to you, but to others I speak in parables, so that, 'though seeing, they may not see; though hearing, they may not understand.'"*
>
> LUKE 8:10

Was knowing the message of the cross a modern-day kingdom secret? Certainly, few I spoke to, clergy or laity, had much of an idea about it, and often not enough to be able to share it. And yet how refreshing it is to discover that it is neither exclusively mine nor my colleagues' nor anyone else's; it belongs to each one of us who is called to partake of it.

So, through the estuary vision, the scene was being

set. The beginning of my understanding about the kingdom, and most importantly my trust relationship with it, had arrived. I have heard it said sometimes that even if there were no rights or wrongs assumed about the way the church does any kind of ministry, we were created by Jesus to work with him in extending the kingdom of God and are accountable for the extent to which we are successful in advancing that kingdom.

But I could now see that this idea comes from a misunderstanding of what is meant by the "kingdom of God". The kingdom itself is not something to be "furthered" or "built on" by our efforts, as I had been struggling to do through all the techniques of healing ministry that the church had been teaching me.

It is something which we are asked to realize as being here already in the life and work of Jesus. It is something that we who believe in Christ should not be actively trying to grow and stretch and give away, as I had been trying to do in the river up to my knees. It is something to inherit and enter into. The role of the church in these matters is not to persuade the world how it might be a better place than it is at present, but to draw a curtain aside from it, to reveal something that is already here.

And so my understanding of the healing ministry completely changed. I had begun to realize that if I drew back the curtain by proclaiming glory to God for the cross, then the Holy Spirit would back me up by flooding the situation with a wake of healing grace.

Chewing over joyful slices of my youth, I recall tidal estuaries and dark-green wooded hillsides, whose overhanging frowns reflect in the water along the river-banks; it is such a pleasing thing to revisit those scenes when time allows. I go back to that place where the estuary vision was given – not only the memory, but the actual place that features in the memory – as often as I can. It was there that more insight came.

Along the edge of the estuary there is a narrow, twisting lane. There is a wall a few feet from my left elbow beyond which is a sheer drop to the water. If I step to the right along that lane and reach out my hand, I touch the front wall of a row of quiet, blossom-covered, pretty, terraced, thatched cottages.

I have always marvelled at my first guide dog. He has died now, but he always marched steadfastly along, watching to left and right, at the same time as looking ahead in case of any obstacle along the way. He was on his best guiding form at moments like this, a feat deserving particular mention and high praise, as the magnetic smell of the river must have invaded every nerve. Was he particularly alert because of the tricky terrain or was he searching every possibility for an escape passage down to the river?

The tarmac lane suddenly slopes alarmingly downwards and comes to an abrupt end. At low tide I would expect the asphalt to peter out on the mud-and-gravel foreshore further down, but the last time we were there the evening high tide was full, and my dog stopped at the water's softly slapping edge.

I dropped the harness handle on to his back to signal the end of his time of duty and he took three steps forward to the extent of his lead, till the water reached his stomach and chest. There he stopped, sideways on and staring straight at me, eyebrows raised in an unspoken question. As easily as one senses someone else's eyes boring into one's back, I had learned over the years of working with him to sense the flickering of his eyebrows.

We stood there for a while, staring at each other and relishing quite different feelings. This was hard for him! All his natural Labrador nature, generations of breeding and genes passing down the line, screamed at him to let go and to throw himself into play. A watery adventure awaited, full of silver spray and deep, dark-green river.

But he could not move. He was locked where he was. He was still wearing his guiding harness and he was fully aware of it. All his nature was shouting at him to go, and all his training was telling him he should stay put – watchful, commanding, mature, sensible, full of self-confidence and authority.

His questioning eyebrows were demanding a decision from me. If I slipped his harness he would be in the middle of the estuary before I could blink. If I called him he would be at my side even quicker. He was wrestling inside. His mind must have been full of turmoil but he stood his ground.

Was it much the same sensation, I found myself wondering, for those poor priests who, under Joshua's command, stood looking at the Jordan in full spate and possibly doubting their own sanity? God had already told them that he had given Jericho, on the other side, into their hands. He had already made his intentions quite clear. They approached the flooding river with the Ark on their backs. It contained the Ten Commandments, the piece of manna and the rod of Aaron that had budded. Everything they knew about God was carried on their backs. Everything my guide dog knows about guiding, his harness and how to handle it, lives on his back.

I wondered if, in the same way that the dog was fighting himself at that moment, so too did those priests fight themselves inside. One wrong move on their part, one careless slip, and everything they stood for, everything they knew and believed about God, would be lost.

They would not be able to control the situation; it would be a total, foot-slipping disaster. Everything would be carried away by the flood. But they knew what to do. They knew how to overcome. They had heard God. One step forward from the first priest and the waters would apparently part for them. Dry land, Jericho and the promised land lay ahead. All that was needed was one giant step of faith.

In the natural world of human common sense, they must have been thinking this one simple move to be indescribably foolish. But hindsight and memory of that event would give glory to God. One could almost say that Jericho was taken because one unnamed priest took his courage, his convictions and the evidences of his God in his hands and stepped into a flooding, racing world of risk. They crossed into the middle of the river Jordan on dry ground.

It was beginning to dawn on me that this was exactly my experience. To become a kingdom walker, to walk naturally up and down in the promised land, to see the children of God inherit the promises, to see regular, consistent, miraculous, Jericho-style wall tumbling – all this requires just one step. It's a dangerous step, an apparently foolish step, but a step of obedience that changes everything.

This is how we can begin to become walkers in the kingdom of God. We honestly take stock of our prayer experiences with God. We recognize that persuading him to heal the sick and the injured supernaturally bears no resemblance to the atmosphere of released freedom depicted in that surfing speed-boat on the river, nor to the flow of ministry seen in the early church.

Anything more than offering quick intercession prayers for the sick is much more like the picture of me standing knee deep in the river, shovelling the badly needed water, a handful at a time, onto the nearest plants. It is hard work, if it is to be faithful and consistent, and it achieves, if truth be recognized, remarkably little.

People would often say to me in those days of initial

discovery, "But how do you know what effect our ministry has? How do you know people are not getting healed?" to which I could only reply, "If they were getting healed like they used to get healed, then the whole world would know about it!"

Of course, we would find it difficult admitting to that, being Christians. Because we know that God is love and God is good, we have to stay in forgetful denial about all those helpless and hopeless times of prayer, those half-hearted prayers thrown heavenward which may help or may just help things not to get any worse!

If we spiritually stood still long enough to survey realistically the whole scene of sickness and injury around us, we might soon find ourselves tumbling into depression at the sight of such volumes of suffering. At the end of any prayer time we look at our watch and go home, believing maybe that we have done our bit. Prayer, we tell ourselves, is all we can do about anything, really.

The death of the remaining plants, the unresolved suffering of the sick, we wash away from our minds – a clever piece of social denial, so that we can get on with life. But we know deep down in our souls that this is a bad place to be. There was a great restlessness about all this in the depths of my spirit. Somehow I instinctively knew that this was not how it should be.

Back at the real estuary's edge, I moved on. I stood a moment longer beside the quietly lapping evening water with my guide dog, wondering what the rich man at his banqueting table in the Bible story (Luke 16:19ff) must have thought of the poor beggar, sitting with his sores at the gate, waiting and hoping for bread. I guess he must have only thought of this sick beggar as part of the landscape, if he saw him at all. He must have gone virtually unnoticed most of the time, as the rich man went in and out of his house.

I could scarcely bear to think what the afterlife of hell must be like for the rich man in Jesus' story. How can a Christian like me possibly allow the sick to remain part of the landscape or ignored, as the rich man did to Lazarus? If I have, as I like to believe, received the Spirit of Christ, then that Spirit must be the agent that burns away and changes my being so that I can begin to gain the mind of Christ.

I knew from my Bible reading that Jesus had compassion for the sick and longed to see the kingdom revealed to their sickness. We can see a description of God's compassionate nature in Exodus 34:6:

> *And he passed in front of Moses, proclaiming, "The Lord, the Lord, the compassionate and gracious God, slow to anger, abounding in love and faithfulness…"*

We can see it too in this incident in Mark's Gospel (1:40–42):

*A man with leprosy came to him and begged him
on his knees, "If you are willing, you can make me
clean."*

*Filled with compassion, Jesus reached out his
hand and touched the man. "I am willing," he said.
"Be clean!" Immediately the leprosy left him and he
was cured.*

I had certainly been finding that praying for people is hard work. Most often we ask, we beg, we cajole, we promise, we make deals with God, and we sometimes even cry out before we give up. When we do give up we quieten our conscience with such human imaginings as God having other plans for the sick person. We remind ourselves that death is the great healer anyway, or that pain is God's way of purifying the soul.

If such excuses do not come naturally to our theologies, then we shrug our shoulders over the next sick person and say to ourselves something like: "Perhaps he really didn't want to be healed after all", or "Perhaps, like being in prison for a long time, he takes some comfort in his illness." If it isn't this that is killing him, then perhaps he has some great unrepented sin that God cannot forgive him for, and therefore God cannot heal him because of its blocking effect.

We could, of course, say only one prayer, tell ourselves that the responsibility is God's now, and move on and away to other things. When it is time to give up the hard work of healing prayer, we silently blame the awfulness of life, and take our aching prayer knees home. We have a God who we know hears our prayers and loves us, but in the matter of healing the sick, I suppose I had always doubted whether he was as consistent and reliable as he used to be.

As a Christian I couldn't ever admit to this aloud, but that is sometimes what our experience seems to tell us, and questions and doubts come. I knew that God was no preferer of persons, but he sometimes heals my neighbour and not me! God, we say, is in control, and then a prayed-for friend dies in a traffic accident. Why so? What sort of a deity would heal one stroke victim and not another? What sort of loving God could not afford an angel to protect a motor car?

I had been avoiding all these nagging doubts and questions, slipping into the easy spiritual denial of calling it all "mystery".

But wait! What happens if I pick up all my experiences of God and take the risk of actually stepping out into the river of man's doubting? Whatever happened to the original Jesus? The Jesus of Matthew, Mark, Luke and John never behaved in that way. He may not have healed everybody, but he most certainly did heal everyone who came to him and asked him. He never said "No." He never told anyone to wait.

No sick person was ever commanded to sort their own lives out first before they could receive healing. He never gave up half-way through. He never discerned the Father's will in matters of healing to be anything other than "Yes" and "Amen". He said that he only did and said what he saw the Father doing in heaven. Jesus is, after all, the only perfect image of the invisible God.

So what would happen if I started to pray, minister and behave as if the Gospel stories of Jesus were actually true?

That would mean hoisting the written word of God onto my shoulders and stepping into the raging waters of my own philosophies and doubts. Not just mine but everyone else's around me as well.

"Take a deep breath," I told myself, "and let's go!"

CHAPTER 9
The Woman and the Dragon

And then the lady had screamed. I had been invited to speak at the magnificent Methodist Central Hall, Westminster, London. I stood for almost a whole day on the same spot on the platform where Gandhi had stood to make his passionate plea to the League of Nations, to set India free.

I was blissfully unaware of this. Instead I had been joyfully absorbed in talking to the inquisitive folk who had gathered there, sharing all we had discovered so far of the miracle-working ministry of the early church and encouraging them to join in. As we were about to break hungrily for lunch, one of the team sidled up to me.

"Mike," she whispered, loudly enough for all to hear so that it became a fait accompli. "It's time to show them. We have to allow God to do his thing!"

So we did. A quiet encouragement to receive from God was issued, and someone came slowly and nervously down the sloping central aisle and stood in front of me.

Her story was a painful one, just to listen to. My radio microphone broadcast her story throughout the hall, but she had agreed to that before we spoke together.

Her pelvic girdle had been crushed in a long-ago car accident, she explained, her voice a little shaky with a mixture of nervousness and the emotions of the traumatic memory. This was, she excused herself, before the days of compulsory seat-belts. Her bone structure had never quite returned to its original shape, leaving her walking slightly lopsided, with all the attendant aches and pains of bad posture.

We stood in the place where the central aisle opens up towards the main platform and I took hold of her hands. Together we began to thank God that Jesus had taken all our pains and carried all our diseases…

I could hear the bones on the move. They seemed to grind a bit and squeak a bit as they came into proper shape and, thankfully, the lady concerned felt nothing. "How does that feel?" I asked her after a while, when the movement of the bones appeared to have stopped.

She twisted her back and bent herself from one side to the other. She bent forwards and she bent backwards and exclaimed, "That's wonderful! It all feels so loose and free! Thank you, Jesus!"

I felt quite elated. These things, in my experience to date, usually happened in other countries, on television and at the hands of especially anointed people. But here it was, happening again and again to me, an ordinary

Christian just like everyone else. God's intervention in sickness in miraculous ways was not occurring once in a blue moon, as one might have expected; it was happening every time we stood up to speak.

That was the clue. Our roles had changed. We had moved from either the invocation of the Holy Spirit or masses of "please" prayers to a quite different prayer position. We were simply proclaiming the good news of the cross and God's kingdom.

We were beginning to work in partnership with our Lord. God, who is always with us, was then healing the sick to prove we were right in what we were saying. We weren't praying, we were proclaiming!

That idea of proclamation, I discovered from Scripture, is not extraordinary at all. Peter, Paul, Barnabas, Philip, Stephen, all these guys were actually doing it that way. Here's two of them proclaiming with joy and watching the sick being healed by God as a consequence:

> *Philip went down to a city in Samaria and proclaimed the Christ there. When the crowds heard Philip and saw the miraculous signs he did, they all paid close attention to what he said. With shrieks, evil spirits came out of many, and many paralytics and cripples were healed. So there was great joy in that city... Simon [a sorcerer] himself believed and was baptized. And he followed Philip*

*everywhere, astonished by the great signs and
miracles he saw.*

ACTS 8:5–8, 13

*Therefore I [Paul] glory in Christ Jesus in my
service to God. I will not venture to speak of
anything except what Christ has accomplished
through me in leading the Gentiles to obey God by
what I have said and done – by the power of signs
and miracles, through the power of the Spirit. So
from Jerusalem all the way around to Illyricum, I
have fully proclaimed the gospel of Christ.*

ROMANS 15:17–19

They were taught by Jesus, later disciples were taught by
the original apostles, and we were just copying what they
had been taught.

Then I heard the scream. It came from high up at
the back of the auditorium and filled me with trembling
and trepidation. I thought, "Is this remote deliverance
ministry? How scary! How can I control something awful
happening so far away from me? Have I lost my audience
altogether? Are they having their own party up there on
their own? Shall we close this whole thing down quickly
and go for lunch?"

I need not have worried. Everything was fine. It was
just more of God's shadow healing going on. Over lunch
the lady who had screamed sought me out to let me know

what had happened.

"Oh, Mike," she said, apologetically, "I'm the lady responsible for the screaming just a few minutes before lunch! Well, actually it wasn't me, it was Jesus. I was born with a trigger finger. In those days you didn't operate but these days I suppose they always would. I was born with this finger bent over like this."

She lifted her right hand to show me, with her index finger bent right over so that it touched the ball of her thumb. "That's how it was when I was born. Forty years ago. My parents always said it can't be straightened, it's just like it is.

"I was watching and listening while you were down the front, praying with that lady from the car accident. As I was listening to you I was moved, I guess by the Lord, to hold out my right hand in front of my face so that I couldn't see you and what you were doing. As I held it up the finger just straightened up. Of its own accord. Just like this!"

She straightened her finger, using it to point to the ceiling. "That's impossible! God has healed me! I'm sorry about the noise. It wasn't me screaming, it was my prayer group. They came with me for the day and they actually saw it happen. They were thrilled. Me, too! How exciting!"

By this time on our adventure down the road to effective kingdom healing we had been getting used to the idea of "shadow healing". Jesus did it and Peter did it. If

Peter did it, then it seems clear that you don't have to be the Son of God to be used in this way. What is it? How does spontaneous healing happen? Peter walked to church in the sunshine one day and all the sick on the pavement stood up and went home healed, without ministry!

A speaking engagement in a convent a month later would give me further insights into how to answer the questions above. If the episode of the trigger finger was not extraordinary enough, there was more, much more, to come. Although it is a kingdom joy that these miracles happen quite regularly, two particular occurrences of shadow healing lie uppermost in my mind as I remember those days of early growth and how exciting they were.

The first of these was Sister Mary's hand. We had been teaching all morning in a convent, sharing with the residents and a group of their families and friends how we see the dynamics of the kingdom working today, expressed originally through the words and works of Jesus. We had spoken only of Jesus from the New Testament, how he saw things, what he did in terms of healing the sick and the injured, and why he would have done these things. As he is the King and everything that happens in the kingdom is according to his will, then we were proclaiming the kingdom again.

Pausing for a light lunch in a private side room, we were introduced by the Mother Superior to Sister Mary with these words. "Sister, would you like to tell our guests what's happened?"

With a completely straight face and displaying no emotion, she related: "I was born with what the Bible would doubtless refer to as a withered hand. It wasn't right at all. I have always worn a glove, not because I was ashamed of it but to save the embarrassed stares of anyone catching sight of it."

She turned to face me. "While you were speaking about the Lord this morning, I felt a tickling in the palm of my hand inside the glove and bent back its cuff to take a peek. The hand is now in all respects exactly like the other."

We were stunned. As we sat around that refectory table with our sandwiches and coffee, the atmosphere was so electric with excitement that I almost wondered if I was dreaming. But, no! This was the real stuff. This was straight out of the Gospel stories. This was a bombshell, a blockbuster! This was a gentle lady with a withered hand. Her religious vocation meant that she would have been familiar with the power of the message of the cross. She had been restored, one hand just like the other.

I couldn't contain myself any longer and threw my arms aloft towards heaven. "Alleluia! How wonderful! God is great! That's just fantastic!"

Sister Mary slowly raised her head from looking at her new ungloved hand, and continued to stare at me stone faced. "Why are you so surprised, Michael?" she asked me in a severe tone, as if she was a headteacher and I was a schoolboy about to be reprimanded. "You should not be surprised at all." She paused for a couple of heartbeats to measure my reaction. "After all, you have been preaching the living word of God!"

I felt very small. She was right! We should expect these things. I sat there shamed into silence while my heart was still rattling and shaking with the thrill of the occasion. I had been taught a powerful lesson – it's the preaching of the word of God as a practical, veritable, living, breathing thing that raises expectation and trust and opens the doors for the kingdom to move into a person's life.

It's our trust that draws God's reality into ours. That is exactly how shadow healing happens. Faith expectancy is a vital component of kingdom dynamics, and faith comes by hearing. Corporate expectancy is raised, praise and thanksgiving begin to take place and God begins to show us his salvation.

The other prominent memory of shadow healing, out of many occasions since, was Lisa. Fifty per cent paralysed from a stroke fifteen years earlier, Lisa had joined one of our kingdom healing courses in the Welsh hill country, in the very reasonable expectation of developing a simple, consistent and reliable ministry in her local church.

Over dinner on the first evening of the course, a member of staff asked her if she had ever been prayed for over the question of her paralysis.

"Oh, no!" she had emphatically replied. "My church says I will never be healed because I used to be a Buddhist."

But God, to everyone's delight, had other plans in mind. Coffee time the following morning found Lisa and I sitting together in the lounge, with a medical doctor and a nursing sister who were also on the course.

"How do you cut your fingernails?" I asked her, for the sake of making light, coffee-break conversation. Her left elbow was bent and fixed through ninety degrees and her fist was tightly and rigidly clenched.

"It takes two physiotherapists to do the job," answered Lisa. "One has to use all her strength to prise open my fingers while the other snips away as quick as she can before they close again. I am bruised for a couple of weeks after they've finished!"

When she left the room before the next lecture, the medics quickly explained the situation to me. "After fifteen years those joints have set like reinforced concrete. Nothing on this earth will shift them now. That's why cutting fingernails is such hard work for her. You wouldn't have seen it, but her left leg is permanently bent at the knee and the foot is turned inwards. She walks on the side of it. That's a brain injury – there's nothing wrong with the foot itself. The brain just tells it that it's bent over."

As if that wasn't enough, they went on to suggest that Lisa might well have had some sort of heart condition, as her lips had a blue tinge to them, and her cheeks were pallid. Her complexion was an ashen grey.

I thought no more of it, having instead to concentrate on the content of lecture after lecture as the course continued on through its lively curriculum. But twenty-four hours later the penny had dropped for Lisa. It had dawned on her that Jesus had never turned anyone away.

He never said "No". He never refused anyone on any grounds at all. He never asked about their religious history as if it might get in the way. He said "Yes" to everyone who asked him. God doesn't change. The nature of grace was beginning to dawn on her as she sat listening to the talks about the kingdom. The Spirit at work in her was proclaiming the good news of Jesus to her soul. And then it happened.

The doctor sitting close to me whispered, "I don't believe it!" He went on to explain, in the hushed silence, that Lisa had begun, of her own accord, to move her arm. She was quietly rotating the elbow around and around, slowly at first and then more confidently in ever-increasing circles, and saying to no one in particular in a tiny, squeaky voice: "I've found a new physiotherapist!"

That evening we prayed with her. We never asked God for anything for Lisa, as Jesus has done a complete work of salvation on the cross. It would be more accurate to say that we spent a while with her in praise and thanksgiving for all that Jesus had been to us and all that he had done for us. That, too, is proclamation.

As we did so, the left shoulder came completely free and the elbow below it straightened, becoming flexible to the point where her hand was hanging easily by her side. The left knee straightened and so did the left foot, and she set off around the room on tiptoe, watched by a silently stunned audience, revolving her shoulder and elbow like a windmill to show it off!

On her return to us in the centre of the room, the doctor whispered again in my ear: "I would think that the heart condition is being healed as we watch. Her lips are losing all the blue and she has pink cheeks!"

When Lisa eventually sat down again in the conference room, the lady sitting next to her proclaimed, "Gosh, it's so hot in here! Can we have the radiators turned off for a while? My back's burning!" Someone looked behind her for a radiator to switch off and couldn't find one. She was sitting in front of the window with her back to a sheet of cold glass. The pain of ten years of osteoporosis had been instantly healed. This is shadow healing. This is God's restoring grace without prayer. This is the work of God, commonplace when the kingdom is being proclaimed.

There are so many other cases of shadow healing that I forget most of them. I don't mind forgetting them, as they are signs and wonders of the kingdom and no one remembers a road sign after they drive past it – they just have to make the right turn so that they finish up in the right place.

I do, however, remember the surgeon who came to a healing service at The Well and approached me for ministry at the end of our time together.

"I have had a vertebra missing in my neck, all my life," she told me. "This means that my neck has always been rigid. I've never been able to nod or shake my head. At my time of life I find it more and more difficult, bending over bodies all day long, like I have to. By the time I get home each evening my neck is aching like billy-o and I really need a stiff gin and tonic!"

But, to my puzzlement, when I offered to pray with her about it, she declined. I raised my eyebrows at her, inviting some explanation. Why had she come all this way to tell us about the problem and then decline our prayers?

"Well, you see, I just wanted to tell you that my neck was healed in the car coming here this evening!" She followed up this staggering statement by gleefully waggling and shaking her head from side to side.

Then there was the lady who could only hear through one ear. The other one had been smacked by a hockey stick when she was fifteen and a perforated ear drum had swiftly led to deafness in that ear. And now she had come to a healing service on her eighty-fifth birthday! When the time for ministry arrived, she got up from her seat, walked half-way down the centre aisle, stopped, turned smartly on her heel and returned to her seat. Afterwards she was thrilled to report that her hearing had been granted back to her, clearly and completely, when she was just half-way down towards us. I so delight in all these stories, as they so clearly demonstrate who is "doing the business".

Towards the end of that blessed time together when Lisa received her healing, I was asked by a course delegate,

"I rejoice that you have the anointing to heal the sick. I want that anointing too. Please will you pray for me and give me the anointing?"

"No," I told him, "you already have it! You should understand this. Only one person has the anointing, and that's the Anointed One! But you have it already, as much as any human being in Christ does, because the whole church was anointed to heal the sick at Pentecost. It's teamwork. It works like this: you proclaim the kingdom, and God does the kingdom business to prove the truth of what you say. You don't heal, you proclaim the kingdom!

"That's how Jesus taught his disciples to do it and that's how I'm teaching you. You can do it too. You don't need to worry about the healing ministry, you need to know how to proclaim. Hold out Jesus to them!"

Then one day my cousin came to call. She is a great lady of prayer and always worth listening to. She told me, "I have a piece of Scripture for you. I was praying for you and this just popped into my mind. It's pretty unusual, not the sort of thing at all that would readily come to mind when you're praying for someone, but here it is."

She read Revelation 12:1–9 to me:

> *A great and wondrous sign appeared in heaven: a woman clothed with the sun, with the moon under her feet and a crown of twelve stars on her head. She was pregnant and cried out in pain as she was about to give birth. Then another sign*

appeared in heaven: an enormous red dragon with seven heads and ten horns and seven crowns on his heads. His tail swept a third of the stars out of the sky and flung them to the earth. The dragon stood in front of the woman who was about to give birth, so that he might devour her child the moment it was born. She gave birth to a son, a male child, who will rule all the nations with an iron sceptre. And her child was snatched up to God and to his throne. The woman fled into the desert to a place prepared for her by God, where she might be taken care of for 1,260 days.

And there was war in heaven. Michael and his angels fought against the dragon, and the dragon and his angels fought back. But he was not strong enough, and they lost their place in heaven. The great dragon was hurled down – that ancient serpent called the devil or Satan, who leads the whole world astray.

She was right! That's not the sort of encouraging Scripture extract that's readily thrown around at prayer meetings.

She said: "Mike, I know this is for you. I don't know what it means. As far as I can find out, I don't think anyone really knows what it means. Perhaps that's because it's all in the future? Anyway, the child in the vision must be Jesus, because the writer identifies it as a son, a male child, who is to rule all the nations with a rod of iron, an iron sceptre.

But as for the rest of it?" She shrugged.

"It seems to be a warning, as far as I can tell. I think you are in the process of giving birth to something which is of Jesus, and the enemy is going to try to snatch it from you."

Well, he certainly did! Within six months I had endured a massive heart attack and was rushed by ambulance into hospital, with Ginnie in hot pursuit.

Scans showed that a significant segment of heart muscle had died in the attack and further examination showed that the arteries supplying blood to the heart were well and truly jammed up with all sorts of undesirable goo.

The surgeon informed me, "You are a very lucky man! About fifty per cent of people having attacks that severe don't make it to the hospital. Someone has snatched you out of the jaws of death! Now, joking aside," he went on, "we can do something about the tubes, that's easy. It's called by-pass surgery. But the muscle…?"

I had the prognosis a few days later. I would have to carry around a dead lump of meat in my heart for the rest of my life. That, I thought, would be truly incapacitating.

One man in particular came to pray with me, for which I felt both relieved and grateful. It was the late Shirley's husband, who had joined us early on this road to the miraculous kingdom life, after his wife had died of cancer. He knew all about expectancy, about persistence, about the humility of prayer, about our kingdom authority, which was so dependent on our sonship. He knew what we'd been learning and what we'd been teaching. He had seen thousands healed through this ministry and he had come to sit on the end of my hospital bed.

We rejoiced together in the cross and its victory over sickness and disease and death itself. Further tests some months later showed that all the dead heart muscle had come back to life. The tubes were still blocked but at least I would not have that weight clinging to the side of my heart for the rest of my life.

One question plagued me while I waited for surgery, but I soon realized the answer. Why, I asked myself, did God heal the heart muscle and not the tubes? Well, that answer wasn't difficult to find.

Romans 12:3 says that we only have a measure of faith. The measure is a gift of the Spirit and is needed to open doors to heaven's healing grace. Thinking about it later, the doctors had told me that they could easily sort out the tube problem but not the dead muscle. So I had put my faith in God for the dead tissue and in the doctors for the bit they could do. Nothing wrong in that; medical science is a great gift of God, after all.

Well, they opened up my chest and snipped the tubes. They took pieces of me from other pieces of me and stitched it all back together again. It felt as though I'd been hit by a truck.

For most of us, thankfully, that's normally the end of the story. But whatever it was that was having a go at me didn't stop there. Having developed one of those hard-to-shift hospital-based infections, I rapidly finished up back in the same hospital ward with a pump hanging out of my chest, which was at work non-stop, day and night for three weeks before the job was done.

But then, as if the dragon's persistence might in the end overwhelm me, the wound refused to heal. It kept on and on producing undesirable tissue which then led to a third stay in hospital and a third operation.

One thing I learned, bedridden for those hospital weeks and idle months at home. One truth came burning through all the fond memories of exciting ministry times. I was learning that, perhaps surprisingly, it should not be my primary aim and object as a Christian to serve the poor, or the sick, or the disadvantaged. Neither should it be my direct aim to convert the world through evangelism or to hasten world peace in some way, through protest or through hard labour.

For any of us, it is not even our direct objective to portray Christ in the world, or to manage buildings, or to care pastorally for the flock, or to attend church regularly, or to deepen our theological understanding.

But it most certainly is our commanded duty to throw all our energies into coming closer to God, to deepen our personal communion with him. Only then do we see what he sees, while we grow in the patience to stand under the cross of Jesus. It is there that we see the infinite glory and love of the Father. It is there that the healing fountains start. There we can freely allow God to do any or all of these other things through us, and of his own accord.

I was already very busy with at least one of these holy activities, but I was in danger of falling into the trap of confusing a gifting for any of these activities with the calling to do it. To exercise a divine gift successfully does not make that gift into a calling – the latter only exists as a reality when it comes as a by-product of our personal communion with the Almighty.

It was a hard time for all of us, very hard. Community nurses came and attacked what was wrong in my chest wound every week for months afterwards, until one day the Christian senior nurse decided it had all gone too far.

She pointed determinedly at my bare chest one morning in the kitchen and said firmly, "That's it! I've had quite enough of you! Now, do as you're told and get healed!"

The following morning there was no sign of the wound. After all those months, it had completely healed over in the night and it was never to trouble me again. The dragon had left.

That episode really made the nurse stop and think and, before long, she was on one of our kingdom healing courses to discover the nature of kingdom dynamics today. She was the nurse who had stood by the doctor and myself and watched with joy as Lisa left her paralysis behind!

At that point, with my health restored and my soul rejoicing in his grace, I began to look to God in the hope that he would, as Jabez had requested, enlarge my territory (see 1 Chronicles 4:10). And he most certainly did.

CHAPTER 10
Back to Eden

"Jesus came to bring the kingdom, and it is the Father's good pleasure that we should have it," I said.

One course delegate stood up quietly and began to walk towards me. He got half-way, and a crack like a rifle shot was heard in the room. "Praise God!" spoke up the man, who then returned to his seat. His shoulder had been weakened some years before through an accident and had never since stayed in place for long. It was as though it was almost permanently dislocated. But God knew and was present to confirm the words I had spoken to them. The shoulder jumped back into place with no assistance from anyone else and, to the man's delight, has stayed there ever since.

Another delegate sat amazed as the work of the cross unfolded before him. He was hungry to see God at work in his own nation, and for that reason I found myself on a deeply stressful plane journey.

The night flight to Johannesburg was endless, uncomfortable, sleepless, dirty, exhausting, bumpy and noisy. Eating the food was like sucking polystyrene. Looking back at my first flight to the southern hemisphere, I cannot find one pleasant adjective with which to describe it. I hated it!

I certainly wanted to be there and I only wished that it could have been done by throwing a switch! The only thing that made me submit myself to that journey was a burgeoning sense of anticipation that great things would come of it. Praise God, they did. Why had I supposed that would happen?

Almost a year earlier we had picked up a very unusual phone call in the office at The Well.

"I'm a minister from South Africa," the caller introduced himself. "I'm here in the UK visiting my son, who is teaching here. He cannot be with me next week so I'm at a loose end. I thought I'd give you a ring to see if anything's going on that I can join in with."

"Well," we had told him, "as it happens, we are running a training course in kingdom healing next week in Llangasty, a retreat house up in the Welsh hills. Would you like to come?"

"Kingdom healing," I explained to him in answer to his brief enquiry, "is not just another method of ministry, another style. God knows there are enough of them! Kingdom healing is modelled on the ministry that Jesus brought with him from heaven, the one he taught his apostles and disciples, and the one which they have been trying to impart to us all down the ages through Scripture.

Why don't you come and see?"

He readily agreed and we made all the necessary arrangements to get him there and back. The Llangasty Retreat House stands by a lake in the heart of the Brecon Beacons, a restored and developed old country rectory nestling in the peace of the foothills at the side of Llangorse Lake. It is a long way from anywhere and has peaceful views that stretch for miles across the water. The sights and sounds of its bird life, the hills beyond and the absence of many motor cars on the local country lanes make it idyllic.

Beyond the house, at the very end of the lane that leads down to the lake, is a tiny and much-loved church whose doors never close. Opportunities abound at Llangasty to spend hours and hours alone with God.

It was not unusual to have someone at Llangasty with us from overseas; we often see delegates from the USA, Canada, Australia, New Zealand and the Middle East, and it is such a joy to see the message of kingdom healing and evangelism spreading together across the world.

This particular course had run exactly to plan, the audience being interested and attentive as I spoke about the kingdom today and the context of the cross within it. It is these key truths that form the background to all effective and transformational kingdom ministry.

By the time that course had come around, I had developed the habit of a type of meditation I had begun to call "Pure Thinking". I am persuaded that this type of spiritual exercise, led by prayer for the Holy Spirit's guidance, will do more to educate us spiritually than any other activity we can engage in. It means starting off an adventurous thinking process by stringing together what otherwise might only be a bundle of abstract ideas, letting one idea give birth to another, and that one to another, until the mind is teeming with them like a lake brimming over with jumping fish.

You compare one idea with other ones, weighing, considering, evaluating, approving, respecting, correcting, refining; joining strings of thoughts together like an architect, until a whole edifice has been created inside the mind. You might travel back in your imagination to the beginning of creation and then leap swiftly forward to the end of time; jumping upwards through limitless space and across the universe, and downwards into an atom's nucleus.

And all this is done without so much as moving from your favourite armchair or opening your eyes to look around – to do this is to soar above everything I think of as the lower creation and to come near to God's angels. What shall we see there?

God begins to reveal to us what lies on the other side of the symbolic curtain between heaven and earth. The Temple curtain in Jerusalem always kept people from the holiest of places, the holiest of sights. None of us, except the holiest of people, could see through it. But it has been split apart by Jesus, allowing us a much fuller access:

And when Jesus had cried out again in a loud voice, he gave up his spirit.

At that moment the curtain of the temple was torn in two from top to bottom. The earth shook and the rocks split. The tombs broke open and the bodies of many holy people who had died were raised to life.

MATTHEW 27:50–52

Here we may really watch the working out of open kingdom secrets and learn to proclaim them into the world that might otherwise be ignorant of them.

"The context in which we find ourselves is this…" I told them one morning after coffee. "In the beginning God created the world, and that story is in the book of Genesis. Now, I don't want to start any trains of thought about whether or not that story is scientifically accurate. I want you to understand that the picture of Eden is like a blueprint. It's God's original idea. It was very good. It's how he wanted it. In his view it's the best. It's how we should be living."

I went on to describe it, both in its known contents and in what is not there in the story. "There is," I filled in the scene, "no war, no hatred, no relationships going wrong, no all sorts of nasty things, and certainly no sickness and no tears. There are no such things in the kingdom of God. Despite what some Christians will tell you, God cannot give you sickness. Sickness is not in the kingdom for him to give!"

Then I talked to them again about the character of Jesus and his refusal to turn anyone away from receiving grace at his hands. He preached the kingdom and healed the sick, and up until his trial that's pretty well all he did. And that's what he taught his disciples.

He did nothing he did not see the Father doing – he was demonstrating the Father's will by healing everyone who came to him. He never said "No". He never said "Wait", he never laid down any conditions or checked up on the wholeness of their spiritual lives first. He gave the kingdom without finding fault. He was bringing in the kingdom. Why? The answer is too simple. He was laying out the divine plan to restore the Eden condition that we so badly damaged for ourselves at the fall.

Here we can glimpse the great purposes of God. Creation is being restored after the mess we have made of it. Here, at the end of history as we know it, we can see the holy city described in John's Revelation eventually coming down to earth and our world being finally restored. What do we find there? No more suffering and no more tears, just the same as the Eden condition:

> … *they are before the throne of God and serve him day and night in his temple; and he who sits on the throne will spread his tent over them. Never again will they hunger; never again will they thirst. The sun will not beat upon them, nor any scorching heat. For the Lamb at the centre of the*

*throne will be their shepherd; he will lead them to
springs of living water. And God will wipe away
every tear from their eyes.*

REVELATION 7:15–17

What part does the cross play in all this? It was on the
cross that Jesus finally took away all that comes between
us and the love of God. It is through his wounds we get
healed because, at the moment of his sacrifice, the curtain
in the Temple was torn in half from top to bottom and
the glassy sea of grace before the heavenly throne burst
its banks.

Jesus himself once commented (see Luke 4:26–27)
that healings occurred only now and again in the Old
Testament times. But God took his hand off the tap at
Calvary. That's when the river of his grace began to flow
down the middle of the golden street in heaven (see
Revelation 21:21), underneath the tree with the leaves
for the healing of the nations (see Revelation 22:2), back
through the torn curtain (or the hole in Jesus' side, if that
picture is easier), and into the world, into this place, into
these rooms in which we sit and all over us. It makes glad
the city of God, where the most high dwells (see Psalm
46:4). And the flow is constant. It never ceases.

At this point I had to stop. The heaviness of God's
presence in the room became obvious to all who sat there.
Strangely enough, it wasn't just a heaviness, but a lightness
as well. There seemed to be a heavy thickness in the room

and yet there was a light, thin atmosphere, as if the weight of glory had descended and heaven was very close. I have come to recognize it as the nearness of the kingdom. He was present to heal, present to demonstrate the truth of what I'd been telling them. There was a hushed silence around the room.

The man we met at the start of this chapter was healed as he made his way to the front. Then straight away a lady stood and came to hold my hands in front of the lectern. "I cannot kneel any more because of my knees," she said.

"Yes, you can," I told her. Standing under the weight of God's presence, there was nothing else I could say. She knelt down on the carpet in front of me, easily, and got quickly to her feet again without experiencing any stiffness at all.

Our South African visitor was, in his words, "gobsmacked". Joyful but stunned. For the first time in his whole ministry life he had actually been present to see the cross at its healing work in the world today. He had spent his entire ministry life preaching about the cross and its saving graces and our love for the one who went through it for us. But he had never been so struck by the reality of the presence of God, expressing his mercies. He would be the first to thank God for it, but he was overwhelmed and has never been the same since.

"If I could get my colleagues to agree, would you come to South Africa?" he had asked. It was his kind suggestion that had led to that exhausting plane journey which was to change so much for so many people.

Once there, after a whole day's recovery from the journey, I met Diana. At the end of our first talk in that country (and there have been many since), she shakily approached the platform and asked me to pray with her.

She had acquired some sort of virus attack in her lower legs at the tender age of eighteen months, which had killed all the nerve ends from her knees to the tips of her toes. Her foot muscles had contracted so that she was walking on her heels with elevated toes but the surgeons had operated on her Achilles tendons, shortening them to flatten her feet on the floor. So she walked towards me like an Australian duck-billed platypus. She was a slender and attractive twenty-five-year-old, bent and buckled and struggling to make the best of life.

We gave glory to God the Father for Jesus. We thanked and praised him for the cross and all that it meant to us. Then she said quietly and with a surprised and delighted tone of voice, "I've got pins and needles in my toes!"

We were doing the holy teamwork. We had begun to give thanks and worship and praise for the cross, and the Holy Spirit was beginning to prove it with signs and wonders of the very kingdom we were bringing close.

She thanked us and left. Now there was a middle-aged couple in front of me, anguished and tearful. "Can we pray for our daughter?" they asked. "She was involved in a car crash and has been in a coma for a month now. They say her brains are scrambled and she will never move or communicate again." They were fighting back the tears. We did not stand there with them, pleading to see God's grace in this family tragedy. We focused on Calvary and all its blessings. We gave glory and thanks to God for the cross and what it means to us.

In the morning Diana came to see me. She had made an appointment to drop in and see her doctor that very morning. A full sense of feeling had returned to her lower legs and feet, the foot muscles had livened and returned to their proper shape, and the Achilles tendons had returned, despite the surgery, to the correct length. She was walking beautifully and most elegantly, as befits a young lady of her age.

And then the middle-aged couple with the paralysed daughter visited me. "How can we tell you this?" they bubbled. "She's coming out of hospital tomorrow! She's awake! She can move everything just as she should! She can't stop talking! She's completely well!"

They burst into tears and so did I. Such utter joy is rarely seen in this world and it's a rare privilege to be present to join in. We slipped easily together into praise and thanksgiving to such a gracious God, and then they told me the rest.

"Everyone else in the hospital ward is going home too. They don't know what's going on down there but everyone around our daughter is better. They're all going home!"

While we were speaking in that church about

kingdom dynamics today and about the wonderful news of the character of Jesus, a number of shadow healings occurred which are fun to remember and fun to relate. One happened on a Saturday morning when we held an open day for other churches in that area of the city. By then the word had got out into the community. They had heard that the presence of the kingdom of God was healing people, left, right and centre. The open day was packed.

A mother and daughter had come together, the daughter unable to carry out her work as a book-keeper because her hands were so twisted, gnarled and pained by a vicious dose of arthritis. I heard them whispering together about half-way through the morning's talk, but I only found out what they were saying later from another lady sitting nearby.

"Mum, look at this!" said the daughter.

"Quiet, dear, I'm trying to listen," replied the mother.

"No, Mum, just look at this!"

"Hush up, will you? How can I hear what the man's saying with you prattling on all the time?"

"But, Mum…"

And then the mother looked down at her daughter's hands. She was holding them in front of her, a few inches above her lap, and there was no arthritis. It had all gone. There were no lumpy knuckles and her individual fingers were flexing easily. I don't imagine they heard the rest of my talk and it didn't matter at all!

At the end of our stay, two important things were decided upon in that church. Firstly, they would create a drop-in healing prayer centre on the church premises and secondly, they would collect some testimonies and publish them to encourage the whole congregation.

There were fifty of them in the first booklet produced. Reports and testimonies had been pouring in of healings which had occurred, some as a result of prayer and ministry during the meetings and services, and others among those simply sitting in the congregation. They were celebrating each of these stories and giving thanks to God for every expression of "healing grace".

The church leadership were also deeply aware that not everyone received the healing they were seeking. They expressed that their deepest wish, as a congregation, would be to continue standing with these folk in their need. Some of their stories included:

> *I have had rheumatoid arthritis in my hands for thirteen years, so bad that I could not even open bottles. A friend invited me to the Friday evening service, where they prayed for me. During the prayer, my hands were very warm, then the joints eased up a bit, not so stiff, and by the end of the prayers, they were tingling. Today they are still tingling, but there is no pain. What a feeling. Praise be to God!*

> DEBBIE

I have an increasingly strange spine, after too many years of running and of course age. This has created pressure on some nerves in my back, resulting in neck and shoulder pain and restricted mobility of my head. I have had this for a number of years, and have had traction, physio and medication, all of which provided temporary and limited relief. I became so used to it that I resigned myself to the fact that I would always have this discomfort. On Sunday morning, I realized that something was different when I was pain free, even while blow-drying my hair which was always a mission. I never told anyone in case the pain returned and I would look silly, but I still have no pain! Besides being really blown away by this, I am of course truly thankful and have begun telling friends and family. Their reactions have been varied, from joy to scepticism, but I will continue giving thanks to Jesus for this wonderful and unexpected gift.

LYNN

In 2002 I was diagnosed with colon cancer. As a result, I had radical surgery and after treatment, went into remission until 2004, when I was again diagnosed with cancer, this time of the liver. After surgery and treatment, I was again in remission until April of this year, when three tumours were found on my lungs. On hearing of Mike Endicott's visit, and long before this most recent diagnosis, I had made the decision to attend his three-day seminar. Mike stated that Jesus said that I had an expectant right to be healed.

After the healing service on Wednesday night, I sent an e-mail to Mike in the UK, telling him of my intention of going for an X-ray on Friday and that I had this expectation of healing. I had the X-rays, and they have revealed that I now do not have the three tumours shown to be present in April, but only one! Praise be to Jesus!

GRAHAM

I have been suffering terribly for the past eighteen months, with very irritated eyes. I have worn contact lenses since 1993, but never had a problem, until eighteen months ago. On visiting a specialist, I was told that these things can and do happen over time. It is called Papillary Conjunctivitis. Big words, but it is a really awful feeling all the time, varying from a gritty sensation, to having mountain ranges in my eyelids. I haven't been able to wear my contact lenses, and as a result of vanity, refuse to wear glasses. Life has not been very pleasant for me these past months.

Now for the good news. After attending the Wednesday evening healing service, my eyes are completely healed, smooth, clear and problem-free! I really praise God for this and still keep on closing my eyes and rolling them around to see if they're still OK and yes, they are 100 per cent. I had not intended attending the three-day seminar, as I've never been interested in healing, but I felt that God was leading me to do it, and I am so grateful that I did. God has ignited a fire in me, that I haven't felt in many years and I don't think that my life or way of thinking will ever be the same again.

HEATHER

During Mike's demonstration of heaven's healing grace with Bertha and Enid on Tuesday afternoon, I was aware of a sensation in my gammy right knee, an old rugby injury. I prayed along with Mike as he had taught us. At the end of the day, I was conscious of complete freedom in my knee. I asked my friends to wait for me before leaving and went over to the church steps. I tentatively climbed the steps and then came down again with no pain and with complete freedom. I repeated the exercise with the same ease, and headed for the car with wonder in my heart. My symptoms started to return on Friday evening and I addressed them in the name of Jesus and they disappeared immediately! All praise to our Lord and his healing power.

DAVID

I have always had a gripping, immobilizing, stiff feeling in my lower back, the result of an injury about twenty-five years ago. I was surfing and hit a rock, breaking my coccyx. The recovery has been very slow. Mike was praying for the healing of someone else's injury on Wednesday and I prayed for myself at the same time, blessing Jesus for his healing power. Over the past few days, I have had the most amazingly mobile back once again. I will continue to bless Jesus for his ongoing healing.

GAIL

My daughter was admitted to hospital yesterday in preparation for a gall-bladder operation today. She was placed on a drip and during the night, praise God, she was healed. When they took X-rays this morning, nothing was found. They again X-rayed and she was clear and discharged without her operation.

LYNETTE

And on it goes, on and on – God's faithfulness lavished on his people, when Jesus' work on the cross is magnified and glorified.

The drop-in healing prayer centre continued sharing the gifts of grace. One lady from a neighbouring town had lost her side-vision as a result of a recent stroke. As she was ministered to she began waving her hands at the side of her face, exclaiming, "I can see my hands again! I can see my hands again!" She expressed her determination to return for further ministry for some of the other effects of the stroke. Her family was overjoyed.

The night flight back to London was exhilarating, joyful, worshipful and full of promise of the coming kingdom.

The joy grows. In the UK, the USA, Canada and many other places, ordinary simple Christian hearts are rejoicing. All the testimonies in this book are first-hand stories; I was there at every event. But the great joy for me nowadays is that I hear just as many stories from the ministries of those who have come to learn about the kingdom.

They have learned about their role in it. They have learned about the cross and gone out and practised its message. There are plenty of folk alive today as a result who can witness to the power of God which touched them through that kingdom message. This is not a new ministry, it's the one that Jesus taught and the one we need so badly to be reminded of.

All this reads as though I might have some sort of special anointing, some special gifting. Is there some way in which God does what I ask, when he doesn't necessarily do that so regularly for other people? Am I more holy than the average Christian? Do I know some special prayers which trigger God to act? How do I exercise this blessing?

CHAPTER 11
An Army of Ordinary People

"Mike," my minder was prodding me in the ribs, "it's eleven o'clock and you're looking too tired. I'm taking you back to the hotel."

He dragged me off the stage and bundled me into a car, where I collapsed wearily on the back seat. In the hotel foyer, just inside the rotating lobby doors, were three leather sofas. Two of them were occupied by two old ministry friends I hadn't seen for years. It was so good to see them.

"We kept a sofa for you!" they joked. "Throw off your shoes and put your feet up for a bit and be with us. Let's chat! A good coffee will get you ready for bed!" It would probably do quite the reverse but I couldn't resist their offer. I lay back with my feet up on the arm of the sofa and took the offered hot drink.

I was feeling pretty exhausted, which was my excuse for being so "laid back" in the hotel. I had taught my greatest joy, the kingdom and the cross, for over an hour at the end of a long day. But the church had not supplied a ministry team. There were over 400 in the pews. The prayer queue was getting longer. I had little chance of getting home that night!

On a back pew had been a lady trying to listen to God. She felt him say to her, "Tonight I will heal you!" She was thrilled. A casualty of phlebitis, she had worn a surgical stocking for seven years, and now, she thought, it would soon be over. She got to her feet and joined the back of the queue, shuffling forward little by little as those at the front, one by one, returned to their seats.

"What will I say to him when I get there?" was uppermost in her mind. The nearer she came to the front the more excited she became, rehearsing over and over again her little speech. The speaker would pray and God would hear him and all would be well!

It was three quarters of an hour before she nearly reached the front of the line. She felt really good, just one more to go. She would tell her story and the godly man would pray and she would be free of years of pain and stiffness. This was going to be wonderful.

She longed to be the subject of this man's ministry. He would know the words to say to God. He was the anointed one with all the practice. God works through him and he would bring healing to her.

It was then that tragedy struck. A man she hadn't seen before approached from the edge of the platform and pulled the minister away! She flushed with anger.

Despair flared up inside. Only one more to go, and she could have been healed. Couldn't he have waited? He is obviously very disobedient, she reasoned through her tears of disappointment. If God was going to heal me through him tonight, then he has prevented that. He has really let me down!

She fled the scene. She ran outside to avoid anyone catching sight of the tears flooding her face. She found her car, jumped in and slammed the door shut, letting out all her rage. She stopped in her hotel car park and pushed the foyer doors open. It was the same hotel where I was staying!

And there I was, horizontal on a hotel sofa, drinking coffee without a care in the world! One sight was enough. She lost control. She flew into a tantrum and through a rage of disappointed tears ran for the corridor and the safety of her room. There she threw herself onto her bed, fully dressed. She fell asleep in a flood of sadness and anger with that "disobedient" speaker.

She woke in the early hours of the morning, completely healed.

She confessed this miracle story to me at the breakfast table. I asked her to jump up with me on the stage that morning and witness to the crowd. She did and she did it joyfully. At the end of her explanation she turned to me and said, "Mike, there's one thing I've found out about all this that I didn't really realize. This is nothing to do with you, is it?"

We all cheered her but no one cheered more than I did. We rejoiced at her revelation.

They rejoiced because kingdom healing, as we refer to it, is for everyone. No individual, no church, no retreat centre is especially anointed to work like this. The whole church was anointed for this work at Pentecost. Do you have to have a calling to do kingdom healing work? Absolutely! But all Christians already have that calling – every single one of us. We are all called to work with our Lord to see his kingdom grow. It's in the Great Commission, given to all of us. It's what he taught his disciples and then he told them to teach it to everyone else. But we've forgotten how to do it!

> *Then Jesus came to them and said, "All authority in heaven and on earth has been given to me. Therefore go and make disciples of all nations, baptizing them in the name of the Father and of the Son and of the Holy Spirit, and teaching them to obey everything I have commanded you. And surely I am with you always, to the very end of the age."*
>
> MATTHEW 28:18–20

He had been teaching them to proclaim the kingdom and heal the sick, and now he was telling us to do the same and teach those who follow us.

But then we worry about our questions: "What do

we pray, what words do we use? To 'get' God to do things for us, which rituals are best? How do we perform so that we don't frighten people away?" We then display a distrust of our God when we ask, "What do we say to them when they don't get healed?"

But all these things fade into the background when a Christian sees the kingdom light. We are not here to have healing ministries, we are here to proclaim the kingdom. When we do it "fully", as Paul has written (Romans 15:17–19), then these signs of the kingdom are made real.

The church today tends to teach evangelism with little or no reference to healing. It tends to teach healing with little or no reference to evangelism. But when we get hold of the idea that it's all one and the same thing, then the world will change around us! ⅄

So here I am, a donkey carrying Jesus on his back, plodding along to victory on the road to Jerusalem. I do the donkey bit and he does the King bit. That's my working partnership with him. I proclaim the kingdom and he does the signs and wonders that bring the words to life. That's Jesus' own healing ministry, the one he taught his disciples. That's what the church's working relationship with him is supposed to look like.

How simple! Those involved with me are continually watching people's world change to the glory of God. They seek to minister Scripture itself, rather than using styles and methods that have grown from it. If only the church could see that the discernment-based and sacrament-based healing ministries of today are not the Light, but shadows cast by that Light.

So many styles of healing prayer revolve around trying to discern what God wants to do about a particular sickness. But Jesus always knew the Father's will and the answer was always the same – "Yes!" And the sacrament-based ministries – that is to say, our inclination to rely on the laying on of hands, or anointing with oil – so often miss the real powerhouse of healing prayer – our humble approach to God that gives honour to him. It's in the message of the cross that the power of God is found (see 1 Corinthians 1:18).

It is not a reluctant God who is hindering the healing of our land. It is our apathy and unbelief that keep us from taking full hold of the potential offered in the gospel of Christ. We should know that entire cities can be saved – Scripture tells us that nations will come to our light and kings will come to the brightness of our rising (see Isaiah 60:1–3). The only thing we lack is Christ-likeness. We have a blindness which hinders us as we seek to follow the master and his ways.

I was much taken with the story of an old Chinese man who left his village for a few months to visit his children in a far-off city. They had become Christians since leaving home. Amid much discussion and prayer, the old man gave his life to Christ and began to enjoy a new life.

At the end of his life-changing holiday he returned

to his village, the only Christian to be found there. Every single day he climbed the hill that overlooked the village and its fields and spent each morning in prayer over them.

"Thank you, Lord, that you have placed me in authority over this village," he prayed. "Your kingdom come. This is your village and you have appointed me to watch over it. Your kingdom come, your will be done, here in this village as it is in heaven."

Over the following few years the rice harvest surprised everyone with its excessive abundance. The farm animals gave more milk and more babies each year. Sickness and disease all but vanished from the village and the people who died first were the oldest, in itself a remarkable change.

Ten years later the old man died and went to glory, leaving the hillside empty every morning. Slowly the harvest yields began to drop back to their original levels and disease and sickness returned to the people. The village elders met to discuss these unhappy circumstances, this change for the worse. They could only conclude, without knowing why, that the good years must have had something to do with the old man who kept faithful watch on the hill above them.

The way I live is a bit too urban to spend my life sitting on hilltops, but it was in the particular context of chiding cities that Jesus said something which unveiled the scope of God's redemptive power. Here is his rebuke, but also its hidden promise. He said:

Woe to you, Korazin! Woe to you, Bethsaida! If the miracles that were performed in you had been performed in Tyre and Sidon, they would have repented long ago in sackcloth and ashes.

MATTHEW 11:21

Tyre and Sidon were Gentile cities known for their debauchery and sin. Jesus said that his life, revealed in power, can bring even the nastiest of cities, places which ought to be destroyed, to "sackcloth and ashes". The strategy to win our cities, therefore, is for the church to reveal Christ's life in power. Yes, the revelation of Christ in us as individuals, and the power of Christ displayed corporately through us, can turn our worst cities back towards God!

Part of the answer lies with the church, with our sins of self-righteousness, indifference and unbelief. The Lord said that if we would humble ourselves and pray, seek his face and turn from evil, he would then heal our land (see 2 Chronicles 7:14). In other words, the future does not belong to the world; it belongs to the transformed church.

Encouraged by the story of the old Chinese man, one day I took stock of my own village. As a kingdom walker, had I been placed in authority over the land hereabouts? I pictured in my own mind a crossroads with a long tail, much like a cross laid on its back, the roads around which the village was originally built. This map in my mind became the extent of my kingdom authority. Like the old Chinese man, I was assuming that God had placed me there to represent my village in the heavenly places. I began to pray the same prayer as he had done on the hillside. It did not take long for the benefits to accrue.

In the crook of the crossbar was a drinking club of a poor reputation. Regular and heavy drinking sessions resulted in much upset in the street outside in the early hours of many mornings. Relationships broke apart that should not have done and many were forged that should not have been. The Godly laws of respect, duty and love were being openly flouted on a regular basis.

But kingdom authority allows, as the old Chinese man discovered, for the right to invite the kingdom to come. I sallied forth on one quieter evening to lay my hands on the building and pray, "Your kingdom come, your will be done in this building just like it is in heaven." And I meant it!

Three months later the night-time disturbances still continued unabated. Sallying forth again to repeat the operation, I was stopped by a neighbour who asked me, "Have you seen the sign?"

He told me that a "For Sale" sign had recently been nailed to the street wall of the building. Exactly three months earlier, the day after I had prayerfully painted the building kingdom-coloured, the company's accountants had arrived to declare the business bankrupt! Nowadays it is still a club, under different ownership, but is now a family place where friends gather to enjoy a quiet drink and each other's company.

The daily prayer of authority continued. Turning left and moving down the main stem of the cross into the body of the village leads us to a public house. This drinking establishment was the place to which teenagers came from miles around to buy drugs. The day after kingdom prayer, the owners came from the city, dismissed the landlord and boarded up the premises for refurbishment. It is open again now but there are no drugs for sale any more.

Continuing down the main stem of the cross, we find another pub which offered drink so cheaply to young people that they could regularly be found lying in the road outside, half undressed in freezing-cold weather, stripped of dignity along with their clothes and intoxicated into unconsciousness.

It is a quiet place now – no teenage drinking to be seen!

Further along the main stem of the cross, the main route through the original village, lay the building used every Sunday by Jehovah's Witnesses. From this establishment they fanned out through the neighbourhood, knocking on doors in their usual style. Significant numbers of people were being converted to their cause. Very shortly after kingdom prayer, they closed down and left the area altogether. The building was taken over by a Christian church.

Still within the boundaries of my imaginary authority

lay three churches of three different denominations, two of which had no pastor. These two quickly overcame all the financial hurdles aggravating their recruitment difficulties and appointed two fine pastors – both kingdom seekers and mighty folk of the gospel and the Spirit.

So how should I leave this story? Am I especially anointed? No more than you. Am I called to this ministry? Yes, but then so are you. So why can't you do this stuff? None of us can.

Consider Elijah on Mount Carmel. He took a huge and exciting risk in front of the king and a large audience of pagan prophets. He built an altar. He hauled his ox up on to it. Did he bring down the fire that consumed it all? No, he must have got out of the way. He must surely have backed off quickly before he got hit by the lightning too!

And that's the church's calling, the reader's and mine. We are called to build altars, to praise God for what he has done in Christ, make thank offerings that honour him – and then back off! No skills needed, no complicated theologies, no addition of secular skills, just thanksgiving and trust.

Lucy had cancer in both breasts. She had thirteen malignant tumours altogether. She and her husband learned to change their prayers from "please" to "thank you". Thank you for healing her? No, not while she was still afflicted: that's too near to trying to exercise mind over matter.

No – they praised and thanked God for the work

of Calvary. They learned enough about the work of the cross to be specific in their thanksgiving. You see, thank offerings honour God and prepare the way for him to show us his salvation (see Psalm 50:23). They kept going. They insisted and persisted in giving glory to God for the cross. No treatment. No surgery. And now no tumours!

And we know God does not show preference. One is just as loved as another. So can you imagine it? Can you imagine what effect the church would have on society if that healing grace could be extended to every cancer sufferer? Can you imagine what effect the church would have in the world if only she went back to Christ's original teaching and began again to administer the kingdom of God?

> *For the Son of God, Jesus Christ, who was preached among you by me and Silas and Timothy, was not "Yes" and "No," but in him it has always been "Yes." For no matter how many promises God has made, they are "Yes" in Christ. And so through him the "Amen" is spoken by us to the glory of God.*
>
> 2 CORINTHIANS 1:19–20

APPENDIX
The Gifts of Calvary

In the story you have just read I've talked often of preaching about the cross and the kingdom of God. The foundations that undergird our preaching and proclamation can be found below. This is an extract from my booklet *Praying the Cross* (The Order of Jacob's Well, 2011):

At the end of his time on earth, Jesus came to Calvary. Everything flows from how we learn the patience to stand under the cross of Jesus, because when we are there we see what he sees: the infinite glory and love of the Father. Calvary is where the healing fountains start, and any understanding of heavenly flowing grace begins with our understanding of the death of Jesus Christ.

What did Christ accomplish on the cross?

Isaiah 53 is the great prophetic picture of the atonement, given 700 years before Jesus' glory-filled death. In verse 6 we read:

We all, like sheep, have gone astray, each of us has turned to his own way; and the Lord has laid on him the iniquity of us all.

We have all turned to our own ways and our own methods of doing things. These are not necessarily God's ways. Natural unregenerate man is born with the stain of Adam's sin, an orientation which has self rather than God at the heart of the human spirit. Until we are born again, our great need is for a Saviour and Deliverer who will put his Spirit within us.

In coming to this earth as a man, God himself makes that provision for all who turn to Jesus in repentance and faith, trusting in him. So it is that Jesus on the cross of Calvary is the focal point for the meeting of all the iniquity of the entire human race. The work of Christ in this stunning place is to redeem us from the curse of the law by becoming a curse for us:

Christ redeemed us from the curse of the law by becoming a curse for us, for it is written: "Cursed is everyone who is hung on a tree." He redeemed us in order that the blessing given to Abraham might come to the Gentiles through Christ Jesus, so that by faith we might receive the promise of the Spirit.

GALATIANS 3:13–14

What curse? What blessing?

What is this great piece of God's business that tears through the veil between heaven and earth in the moment of Jesus' dying? Slung in the utmost vulnerability between thieves, and exposed to the mockery of the world, an exchange between two things takes place before our gaze: cursing and blessing.

So what is this curse of human disobedience and all its evil effects, which was placed upon Jesus on the cross?

> *However, if you do not obey the Lord your God and do not carefully follow all his commands and decrees I am giving you today, all these curses will come upon you and overtake you: You will be cursed in the city and cursed in the country. Your basket and your kneading trough will be cursed. The fruit of your womb will be cursed, and the crops of your land, and the calves of your herds and the lambs of your flocks.*

DEUTERONOMY 28:15–18

As Jesus hung on the cross, he actually became that curse, and it died with him. He completely destroyed the curse so that you and I might become the blessing. Jesus, the eternal Son of God, on the cross, took upon himself all the punishments that were due, in all justice, to the entire human race. Adam and all his descendants, including you and me, were included. In return, the one who believes in Jesus Christ may receive all the blessings of God's kingdom – rather than eternal death.

> *Surely he took up our infirmities and carried our sorrows, yet we considered him stricken by God, smitten by him, and afflicted. But he was pierced for our transgressions, he was crushed for our iniquities; the punishment that brought us peace was upon him, and by his wounds we are healed.*
>
> ISAIAH 53:4–5

The five Gifts of Calvary

Gift 1: Peace

Our punishment was exchanged for God's peace. As he died, Jesus bore the punishment that was rightly due to us for our transgressions and all our iniquities, our acts of rebellion. All the punishment for every contrary act committed by every member of the entire human race was brought on to Jesus. Not one sinful act was left out.

The blessing now available, the alternative to eternal punishment, is summed up in the word "peace". In place of punishment, there is peace for the believer, reconciliation and pardon; and God's justice was satisfied at Calvary.

> *But now in Christ Jesus you who once were far away have been brought near through the blood of Christ.*

> *For he himself is our peace, who has made the*
> *two one and has destroyed the barrier, the dividing*
> *wall of hostility...*

EPHESIANS 2:13–14

Gift 2: Abundance

Our poverty has been exchanged for God's riches. This is the poverty with which we were cursed in our disobedience:

> *Because you did not serve the Lord your God*
> *joyfully and gladly in the time of prosperity,*
> *therefore in hunger and thirst, in nakedness and*
> *dire poverty, you will serve the enemies the Lord*
> *sends against you. He will put an iron yoke on*
> *your neck until he has destroyed you.*

DEUTERONOMY 28:47–48

The curse of poverty, broken down into its component parts – hunger, thirst and nakedness – adds up to a state of total and absolute destitution, and that curse came on to Jesus too:

> *For you know the grace of our Lord Jesus Christ,*
> *that though he was rich, yet for your sakes he*
> *became poor, so that you through his poverty might*
> *become rich.*

2 CORINTHIANS 8:9

Jesus took our poverty on to the cross so that we might have his riches. He was hungry, not having eaten for almost twenty-four hours. He himself said, "I thirst." He was naked, for the soldiers had taken all his clothes for themselves, casting lots for his seamless robe. He was totally bereft of everything, a picture of total poverty, exhausting the curse. Jesus, who was rich with heaven's riches, became poor on the cross, so that we might in turn share in his riches. This is the grace of God:

> *And God is able to make all grace abound to you,*
> *so that in all things at all times, having all that*
> *you need, you will abound in every good work.*
>
> 2 CORINTHIANS 9:8

This is amazing abundance. This is the level of God's provision through Jesus Christ, as a direct result of the cross. God is able to make all grace abound towards us and it comes only through Jesus Christ, because of the cross.

Gift 3: Everlasting life with God

Jesus has exchanged our mortality for a share in his immortality:

> *But we see Jesus, who was made a little lower than*
> *the angels, now crowned with glory and honour*
> *because he suffered death, so that by the grace of*
> *God he might taste death for everyone.*
>
> HEBREWS 2:9

Jesus, our substitute, has tasted everyone's death on Calvary, the punishment due to all of us, because the wages of sin is death. He has paid our wages by his atoning death because:

> *God made him who had no sin to be sin for us, so that in him we might become the righteousness of God.*
>
> 2 CORINTHIANS 5:21

Jesus has died as our representative, on our behalf. He has tasted death so that you and I might have eternal life with him:

> *For God so loved the world that he gave his one and only Son, that whoever believes in him shall not perish but have eternal life.*
>
> JOHN 3:16

Jesus has paid the final penalty for our breaking the law, which is death. He has tasted death for each one of us. He drank the bitter cup to its dregs, the cup of which he said:

> *Abba, Father… everything is possible for you. Take this cup from me. Yet not what I will, but what you will.*
>
> MARK 14:36

In fulfilling the Father's will, Jesus drained the bitter cup of death to the last drop. He exhausted death and by doing so has victory over it, and has made immortality available to the believer.

Gift 4: Righteousness

Through the work of the cross we have been offered Christ's own righteousness in exchange for our own efforts to be holy:

> *For we know that our old self was crucified with him so that the body of sin might be done away with, that we should no longer be slaves to sin...*
>
> ROMANS 6:6

> *But seek first his kingdom and his righteousness, and all these things will be given to you as well.*
>
> MATTHEW 6:33

The difficulty for all of us has always lain in the fact that the only righteousness acceptable in heaven is the righteousness of God. This can now be received through faith in Jesus Christ as the direct result of Calvary:

> *All of us have become like one who is unclean, and all our righteous acts are like filthy rags; we all shrivel up like a leaf, and like the wind our sins sweep us away.*
>
> ISAIAH 64:6

Without faith in Jesus Christ, all we might ever be able to do would be as filthy rags, whereas what all of us need is God's righteousness – which we have in his sight when we receive new birth, made possible by grace through faith, as a result of the cross. God requires that we do not depend on those filthy rags of our own religious activities and good works but that we acknowledge we are sinful, believe Jesus paid the price for our sin on the cross, receive him as Saviour and Lord – and so become clothed with his righteousness.

Our old, naturally rebellious, naturally self-orientated human nature was crucified with Jesus. He, himself, experienced that old human separation from the Father. He underwent that for us so that we should not have to live in that terrible state for all eternity. The way out from under a life of sin is to know for yourself, personally, that on the cross that sinful nature was killed.

There are so many ways in which we try to work out a salvation for ourselves. Some of them are religious; some are based on a misguided belief in human philosophies or confidence in people or good works. But we cannot change the nature of the rebellious heart of mankind. No programme of human reform will ever achieve that. God's provision for dealing with sin is simple: execution. In truth, that remedy has already taken place. As Jesus died, our old, rebellious nature died in him.

Here is the miraculous exchange: that as we receive Jesus by faith as our only Lord and Saviour, the old nature dies. A new nature, a Christ-like nature, a more transparent life is given to the new believer. The nature of Christ then indwells the believer's heart:

> *Therefore, since we have been justified through faith, we have peace with God through our Lord Jesus Christ, through whom we have gained access by faith into this grace in which we now stand.*

ROMANS 5:1–2A

Gift 5: Healing

Our sicknesses and pains have been taken on the cross so that we might receive healing through Jesus' wounds. He suffered terrible flogging and the imposition of the crown of thorns, and was crucified. As those terrible wounds were inflicted, so the covenant remedy for the pains and sicknesses of the whole human race was given. In accepting those wounds, he has made provision for our complete healing.

Two apostles who walked with Jesus, Peter and Matthew, clearly believed healing to be a work of the cross. They both quoted Isaiah in this context:

> *Surely he took up our infirmities and carried our sorrows, yet we considered him stricken by God, smitten by him, and afflicted. But he was pierced for our transgressions, he was crushed for our*

*iniquities; the punishment that brought us peace
was upon him, and by his wounds we are healed.*

ISAIAH 53:4–5

Matthew then connects healing and the cross:

*When evening came, many who were demon-
possessed were brought to him [Jesus], and he drove
out the spirits with a word and healed all the sick.
This was to fulfil what was spoken through the
prophet Isaiah: "He took up our infirmities and
carried our diseases."*

MATTHEW 8:16–17

He may not here be directly referring to the cross but
he quotes Isaiah, and would have known that he most
certainly was.

The second apostolic witness is quoted in 1 Peter
2:24:

*He himself bore our sins in his body on the tree, so
that we might die to sins and live for righteousness;
by his wounds you have been healed.*

Two apostolic witnesses, combined with Isaiah's generally
accepted prophetic description of the work of the cross,
should convince us that healing comes to us through it
and because of it.

Healing is a Gift of Calvary.

Salvation is made up of all five Gifts of Calvary.

On the cross was a bleeding, torn, wounded body, bereft of all things, who took upon himself the punishment due for all our sins, as well as our curses and our poverty – all this so that we might be forgiven and reconciled with the Father, as well as inheriting his peace, receiving healing, deliverance from evil, and abundant life.

So Jesus said: "It is finished."

Home Base
Headquarters

The Welsh Revival came to our part of Wales in 1904. This was not a revival occurring around enthusiastic preachers but a revival based in prayer and promoted by the Holy Spirit alone.

Men and women suddenly fell to their knees in the streets, totally convinced they should get quickly to a church to confess their lives. Our local fishing fleet, having set sail for the fishing grounds an hour earlier, found by common consent that they had no option but to turn all their boats around and step ashore in search of the nearest church.

In this part of the world the churches were baptizing up to 2,000 a week. That's revival! Their buildings were full to capacity, with much singing and weeping and loud confession of sin. Their pulpits were filled with the message of the cross and signs and wonders of the kingdom were commonplace. Out of those churches marched many missionaries who travelled the world with that message.

Someone tried to help with the local shortage of pews. They bought a little land and erected a corrugated iron tabernacle to help contain the crowds. Then, in 1935 they pulled it down and erected a brick building in its place.

After the Second World War it became a central point for local business to advertise employment vacancies and for some years it reverted to being a church again. And then we found it, empty, derelict, desolate, forgotten.

Now The Well Centre in Cwmbran, South Wales, in the UK, is the trembling heart of a busy ministry, studying, preparing materials and teaching the kingdom and its dynamics to ordinary everyday Christians worldwide. It is also one of a number of Wells around the UK fulfilling the roles of the Order of Jacob's Well, ready to listen to, and pray for, the local community.

Nowadays The Well Centre, headquarters of the Order of Jacob's Well, is a prayer and teaching resource centre serving Europe, Africa, Canada and the USA. You can read more at www.jacobswell.org.uk and visit our outreach website at www.simplyhealing.org

For any further information please call: 0044 (0) 1633 483660.